5-99
G

Where the Land Gets Broken

Where the Land Gets Broken

Walter Hildebrandt

Ekstasis Editions

National Library of Canada Cataloguing in Publication Data

Hildebrandt, Walter
    Where the land gets broken / Walter Hildebrandt.

Poems.
ISBN 1-894800-50-8

    I.†Title.

PS8565.I4335W46 2004   C811'.54   C2004-901510-9

Acknowledgements: The author thanks the Alberta Foundation for the Arts
for support during the writing of this book.

Published in 2004 by:
Ekstasis Editions Canada Ltd.   Ekstasis Editions
Box 8474, Main Postal Outlet   Box 571
Victoria, B.C. V8W 3S1   Banff, Alberta ToL oCo

Where the Land Gets Broken has been published with the assistance of grants
from the Canada Council for the Arts and the Cultural Services Branch of
British Columbia

to the memory of Juergen Doerr
brother, mentor, friend

Contents

Outlier:

1a)   One who lies
       sleeps or lodges
       out
       i.e. in the open air
       or away
       from a place with which he is
       connected
       by business or otherwise

       comers and goers

One that lies outside the pale, an outsider

c)   An animal that lies outside the house,
         fold or pack;
            esp. an outlying deer

2a)   "A stone not taken from a quarry,
       but lying out in the field
       in a detached state"

       a boulder

          also outlair

A portion or mass
        of a geological formation
        lying in situ
        at a distance from the main body
        to which it originally belonged
        the intervening part having been removed
        by denudation.

generally
    an outlying portion or member of anything
    detached from the main mass, body,
    or, system to which it belongs

3a)   Fishing. A set line

                  out-line

    a guard ship lying out in front of a port

Moose Jaw 1999

Moose Jaw lies
above and beyond
its origins in enterprise denied

      Saw Capone last night
      second time he'd been seen
      checkin' out the system
      brought in Charlie (sworn to secrecy)
      to give him a haircut
      in a room along one of the tunnels
      comes out on River St.
      streams of whiskey
      flowing all the way to Chicago

The Chinese
working underground
subverting city fathers
circumventing laws and regulations
capitalizing
on marginalized identities
huddled in cramped rooms

Tunnelling to legitimacy
hidden from the streets' gaze
the bow and shuffle
in subterranean beginnings
purchased
with false I.D.'s
(from those who thought they all looked the same)
and let out onto the prairies
along railway lines
they built
to open up the laundries and restaurants
that dot this fragile landscape

step differently now

Less confident about what this smooth pavement covers up

Stirred by a restless conscience
removing the gauze
layer by layer
that covers the trunk and limbs
of this all too seamless history

Stairs
for Juerg

I keep adding
to the beginning/to my beginning
Brooks in the 50s
pouring a foundation
on the outskirts next to the blacksmith's shop

The day stands out
Because you remembered

Returning now so many years later
you told us
how it was
sheltered in our enclosed basement
in chaos/a labyrinth
I remember looking up for the light
and slowly I continued to begin to remember
the steep stairs leading to the not yet completed
main floor
of our underground dwelling

You couldn't find the house at first
so much around it had changed
the upstairs eventually completed
but the once open field across the dirt road
had become a seed factory
and the blacksmith's shop
an antique store

We knock
the lady who now lived
in the house
lets us in
Sarah tells me later
that the weight our faces carried
grew
as we looked around the
basement
where the kitchen was
the toilet the bedrooms
we talk about how the door out had changed
as we search for the place
where the entrance used to be
much had changed
and much stayed the same
like Brooks itself no longer really
recognizable/booming with
the non-union hog plant the oil discoveries
a classic Alberta story

On arriving in Calgary
you brought us
the just completed
Encyclopaedia of Modern Germany
that you had worked on for so long
it is a careful exhaustive work
you remembered
few friends from those early days in Brooks
and the dust
the mud at the end of the wooden walk
a run-down apartment suite across the alley

where we lived as other parts of our house
were being built
we circle the house
wondering again where exactly the entrances were

You gave me the chance to remember
as you talked about
the steep stairway
to the main floor
carefully explaining where
everything was
I then remembered
climbing those stairs
and now see
             all this
wobbling up

as another entry for modern German history

15th St.

to the memory of Juerg

Your best moves were the head fakes
    the quick zig zags
        trying to get open

The grass was fast
    faster even than the fake
        artificial turfs of today

On the cool moist almost dark evenings
    we flew across the lawns like deer
        or dogs with pinned-back ears

Intoxicated by the cool air   lungs aching
    from the endless
        quest for touchdowns

We dangled down the sidelines
    with the elm trees along the boulevard
        as stationary defenders
            you had to account for

The alley next to our house was
    one end zone
        the driveway between the McBean's
            and the MacGowan's the other

And there was the low hedge there
    that you had to jump
        if you went into the end zone too fast

And that was the field – our house
    the driveway the Boomhower's and
        the McBean's

I thought we entered another world
    when we played those games
        hour after hour
Bob Speed Doug Boomhower Dale MacGowan
    Ralph you and I

We became Atcheson, Etcheverry
    Rote, Lancaster, Spaghetti Legs Parker
        The China Clipper, Wlasiuk, Ptacek
           Tripucka, Ferdy Burkett

And sometimes there was what
    appeared to be a crowd watching
        Theresa Heisler, Susan McBean, Margrit
        and I thought I was one of those
           pros being cheered along
Kids seemed to be everywhere in that neighbourhood

And old friends the Horlicks, the Woods
    and scarry Mr. Bossarte
        across the street
           where it was thought
               you would never be seen again
                   if you got caught in his yard
                     this bachelor who worked for the CCF

And then that ended
    we all moved away
        to school
           to the States

But for those few years
    I thought our little war-time house was the center
        of the universe

The launching pad for our dreams and wishes
          we moved around the world in a Beetle
                garter snakes inhabited the high grass
                      along the alleys outside the fence
                            we feasted on the "sweet" crabs
                                  from McBean's tree
                      and the raspberries and strawberries
                and carrots pulled from the lush earth
                of the garden Mom and Dad
                            so carefully tended

It seems like such a brief time now
          a precious place
                to come from

          "shinny" under the
            streetlights in winter
          "catch" through the
            summer
          it seemed we couldn't get enough of it

But for some reason it was the football
          at Murray Park or across our lawns
                I remember most

And at night
          listening to the Roughrider games
                on the radio
All the names of those players I thought were gods

And at the Hilltop games you took me to
        I walked on air
               after getting autographs when the games ended
                  as the players were getting onto the buses
               at Griffith Stadium
Marisi – Beylak – Werezak – Matheson

And I remember
    after finishing papers
        I would go to watch
           the Huskies practise till the
              lights came on
                just across from
                  Stan Graham's place
                    Stan and I watching
                      the drills for hours.

I remember once coming home
    from Brunskill and George Werezak
        was in the park practicing his punting
    and I ran after one of the punts
        returned him the ball
           and he played catch with me
              for a few minutes
    I was stunned speechless
        and on the way to heaven

And that was it
    all that life
        all those hopes and horizons
Saskatoon in the late 50's and early 60's

You lie mostly quiet now so far away in Fredericton
    so distant from those late evening
        dew flecked lawns
           we raced across
But those times will be with us forever
        timeless
           immemorial

I see you still
    in your long sleep and mine
        zigging and zagging across the lawns of 15th St.

Figures racing across green fields
      and it seems always
           playing well into the dark

To the Hills

On this paved road
I drive
to the hills again
Deer cross the road
On the post an owl
A distant coyote
moves
behind barbed wire
        The ever
                    circling hawk

Here wolfers
sodden drunk
swept like thirsty fire
across an Assiniboine camp
in some mistaken revenge

Solomon and Farwell
came here to take what
they could from this now dying buffalo land
where poisoned carcasses
enticed wolves
        with their worn beauty.

Strange, tall lodge pole woods stand above
rich green grasses that spread across last year's wallows
renewed from a black earth
once fire fed
and the hot
lush earth returned
this light spring cover

Battle Creek, Cypress Hills — Night of June 1, 1873

In Cree legend Iyas destroyed the world with fire to avenge the mis-
treatment of his mother by a step-father, she was forced to do hard
work and sleep with the dogs. When the fire died out Iyas turned his
mother into a robin which is a sacred bird to the Aboriginal people.
Iyas told her to fly about to sing and pray for Indian people. Iyas
then turned himself into a toad.

They're coming again

The Americans
     for gold furs hides money

Bringing
     steamboats democracy trade goods death

Brought their business
           to our hills

     and poison

        strychnine for the wolves

Men let loose
     after their civil war

   came killing
     wolves buffalo and men

After the massacre
     they took women

30
died
in early
spring
during
the terrible
starving time

They shot 20 30 starving Assiniboines

Two years later
      one woman

         told them

When I and my daughter
were leading her husband (Little Soldier)
to the fort
he saw his father dead.
He threw up his arms and . . .
turning to them said:

     White men
     you will know what you have done today
     You never knew
     a Woody Mountain Assiniboine Indian
     to harm a white man

at that moment he was shot
through the heart
by one of the party of Americans . . .

Little Soldier's head
impaled
on a pole

trophy
raised
the men
set about
looting and destroying
the camp

The fighting ended.
But wolfers continued
their orgy
captive
Assiniboine women
raped
throughout the night.
Little Soldier's wife
later told
she and others
repeatedly assaulted.

On returning to the camp
One Assiniboine recalled

After dark
I went into the camp
and saw
a woman
with her back broken;
she was still
alive
and was trying
to move
but could
not.
That was all
I saw. . .

40 lodges
left
carrying everything
on their backs
all the dogs having run off.

> *We started*
> *in the night*
> *for the end*
> *of the mountain,*
> *to the half-breeds*
> *they treated us kindly*
> *giving us dogs*
> *kettles*
> *and other things . . .*

The next day traders at both posts hastily finished packing. The wolfers agreed to stay until this was done and busied themselves by burning the remains of the Assiniboine camp. Farwell's Crow wife, Mary, obtained the release of the captive women from Solomon's post. There Ed Legrace was buried that morning under one of the floors. The traders then pulled out and the wolfers rode off to continue the search for their missing horses. As they departed someone set fire to the two posts. The valley was thus left deserted except for the dead Assiniboine who lay where they had fallen.

News of the massacre did not reach Ottawa until late in August. The government soon initiated steps to have those involved extradited from the United States and tried for murder. The case languished for a while and then was taken up by the North-West Mounted Police. Five wolfers were arrested and brought before an extradition commission in Helena, Montana, in July 1875. Farwell was the chief witness for the prosecution and much of the defense was an attempt to prove he was a known liar. The wolfers claimed it was Farwell who led them to the Assiniboine camp, their intentions were entirely peaceful and that they had only fired when fired upon. As it turned out the prosecution case was not strong enough and the men were released. Soon afterwards two traders and a wolfer were arrested in Canada. They were tried in Winnipeg in June 1876. Once again the government case was weakened by insufficient or contradictory evidence and the three men were acquitted. The case was finally dropped in 1882 when it was apparent that no new evidence would come to light.

and when the huge
fires blazed
in the hills
they ate everything
that grew
it raged
for many days
leaving
nothing

Some
said
Iyas
had returned
and shot
four flaming
arrows
north south
east west
destroying
all those
who did
not seek
the shelter
of islands

Others
said the distant screaming
heard
when the
fires
scorched
the hills
was
the cry
of eagles

escaping

In the Shadows of the Cypress Hills

a going back
a return to old
stories
that left us
with what we see
on main street
no longer whole
before narrative

blurred
    returned
fragmented
broken down seen
a/new recognized
an open eyed

    Angelus

        flying

      looking

backward
and for/
word
beginnings

citings

Pasquah (The Prairie)
dreamed

a frog asked the buffalo
who was stealing
fish from the great prairie lakes
that had fed
all who walked and flew
and the buffalo asked the bear
and the bear had heard them
and understanding language
he told them about the dwarves
who filled their canoes each night
the Cree stopped them
gave them some meat
and sent them away
the dwarves travelled
to the shore laughing
and threw the meat into the lake
the rat and the raven
                watching

drenched

        Pasquah

awoke

   stirring

vermilion

     streaming

        thick

campfire

          smoke

still

   rising

they framed us

       drew us
             lower

   beneath

lined us up

     at the edge

           placed us
in square pictures
covered us with glass

      framed

        hung us

    inside
           on
walls

            wrote on square
     white pages

                  long thin lines

                       black

          filed
     in cabinets

                  we carried our

          colours
                       said what we had to say
open
     drew
                  on uneven
animal hides
     scattering

we gather together again

approaching
      this grey
           lake

white caps
         peak

    and fall

rusty swings

  squeal
        steal on steal

  rocket slide

     into dust

   vestiges

of space age

     imaginations

  children squint

 in seething heat

    dirt

   sticking

    to throats

  everywhere dry

Cypress Lake 1985

this is the lake
that began
it
forward
into the past
the fire raging
a hundred years
an ancient place

       traces in the air of that
       three legged coyote
       on his winding road
       to the lake

where caked and
brown red
farmer's blood
collected in a ditch
furrows
of cemented soil
where tattered clothes
no longer keep
the birds away
and scarecrows scare men
scarecrowmen
face down
on spiked wheat

rows neat even
lines where
seeds hope
returned as four
inch spikes
from grey-brown
earth
watched
by the men of Ponteix Cadillac
Eastend Val Marie
men with promises
of the bible
of the god
of the land
go forth
and multiply
no word of drought
in bible
green looks grey
on the rolling hills
distant Vs of dark thick bush
fecund earth
tinder dry
fuel

The earth's yellowed hair
lay flat and dry
in the year before
the great fire
and Riel rose

and Imasees
led the young
against those
hated gov't men

and the black robes
with too many dead words
with dried bread
you cannot
speak down to young strong willed men
young men who have
stood still
watching old men
trying
denied food from Quinn
eyes spitting
hands clenched
boiling up old
salt pork
that wouldn't stay down
young women
taken in the back room
for canned oysters and bread
young men hurting
hating
beyond words

Big Bear who knew fire
waited
even as they starved
by the lake
under the hills
 his daughters mocking him
for this grim destitution
fish eating
Little Pine
fought the Blackfoot
trailed buffalo
in the hills
of winter
no fish eaters
seeing
patterned ribs of children
bickering
ugly now

there had been fire
in the hills
an omen
as Big Bear
the Ojibway
knew

I see him
at the side of the lake
Big Bear stalking

a small groups of tents
beyond the boat launch

revelations looming

the heat shimmering over the land

unsettled air

swings twist in gusting wind
iron chains
dance and rattle
in this now abandoned playground

all listened
at the trail
where he makes them laugh!

we left beads behind
in gratitude
for ochre leaves taken
then mixed and rubbed the burning colours
into our drums tents clothing
dreamed forms
turning in
twisting rising
smoke

red
giving life
always above
black lines of anger sorrow death

in fire
we see how red and black
together
changes everything
nothing stays
the same

torrents of fire
sweeping through the hills that year
eating the Cypress trees
the flames
 levelling
the police post
we were drawn
repelled we laughed and cried

scenes
remembered
patterns
passed down
rekindling
red and black
many thousand years old
we dreamt
in those dark forests
animals talked to us
their spirits
in the shaking tent
laughed at Wisakedjak
raven coyote
spring no
laughing matter
no trick
moving to the open Plains
yet amid want here above thin trees crackling
in the hard stillness of huge blue winter nights
green lights dance below silver stars
in deep sleep dreams from long ago returned

We knew things would go wrong
before Macdonald
and a year after the fight
The Creator let the great forest
burn
the place of magic
and story telling
became a tempest
of roast flesh
the smell
awful and no human
eyes could watch as
tall lodge poles
cracked with pines
fire feeding
a hell of frantic screaming
flame chased
animals
the tall slender poles
for our lodges waving
torches in the huge hungry winds
that swept and swirled
in the dry meadows
this way and that

we knew a thing
was wrong
more wrong than
any one man could
understand
at the
rock
pile
we
went
to see
what
spirit
would be
given us
after
the great fire
it was all
a waste land
for months ground
too hot to walk on
small fires burning
here and there

Laurie wanted it   safe

    a vision of the west

      safe /

         for settlement

  a white West

      safe for / some

      safe from/

            some

  obstacles

         impediments

   civilization

         to be settled

   left   safe

          hanging

    to make the West

    safe

         for and against

We could not sign the treaty
they did not care
for buffalo
they would not
keep wolfers
 from the land
they did not know
the spirit of the
land
they had not sat by
prairie lakes
to love our
great round women
bent from the waist
washing
in the lakes at night
naked warm
wet bodies
taking in
moonlight
who will remember
the love of these
beautiful women
punished in your fury
the weak ones the poor ones

I can hardly believe
those words now
but they were from
the heart
Those words spoken
as you look a man in
the eye
All those other words
on paper
We saw what written words meant
at Pitt and Carlton
We saw
what happened
to a great free
people on reserves
surrounded by
men with paper promises
they would not keep
We saw words from men
in the east
surrounded by lies
Good ones like
Jefferson were embarrassed
men who
did not believe the lies

Yellow Calf   Incident
        made it clear
              just

  how much had failed

     Arrest ringleaders

       thought the mounties

knew starvation led to confrontation

        war dance

the police sought out Louis O'Soup (Osoop: Back Fat, Eng.)

            Qu'Appelle Saulteaux

O'Soup told them

*... that the Indian was
an animal who did not
think the white man in
his wisdom could look
far ahead, but the
Indian reasoned thus –
if he were allowed to
starve – he would die –
and if he were doomed
to die he might as
well die one way
as another.*

Mounties warned

      Indians

          that the Queen

don't allow no free ride here

                    no one to escape trial

      advised

     to give themselves up

      had broken the Queen's law

O'Soup told them again

... when they stole
the provisions their women
and children were starving
and the men we wanted
would not allow themselves
to be arrested – that they
would fight to the death –
that they were well armed
and might just as well die
than be starved by the government.

years later

Louis' buddy Alex Gaddie

    on the way to Ottawa

told Louis to ask the Queen

        for medical assistance

    told him

to ask for a "peg leg"

    a leg to stand on

      he'd lost one

in a railway

      accident

wanted the artificial

    limb

"to come home

    with a leg

on which he will

    be able

      to walk about."

a leg to stand on

What about those
I saved at Frog Lake
warned
against the fury
of the young dogs
wandering spirit
and Imasees
whose hatred went
beyond all bounds

They had not hunted
for seasons too
many to count
they had not seen
the dances to the prairie chicken
or the Sun Dances
when we crawled
out of winter
to wash our thin
souls in the rays
of the sun
when the young
would ask for spirits
to guide them

For me
to stand back like
a bear
and speak
to eat what berries there were
to protect
to sleep through the cold
in spring to scoop fish
the spirit warm not angry
Yet now the burning
the lines encroaching
on our hills
the words
backing us up
always with fewer places to
turn
We loved those rivers
the campfires at night
the gold and red of autumn
the smell of buffalo shit
the taste of hot buffalo livers
the diamond speckled grass of dawn.

That was
a sad day
to arrive at Pitt
to see my brothers sign
that paper
the wretched priests
wanted so badly
brothers led away
That company owned them
now the priests would own them
too
They should have waited for us
we would not believe
the soft whispers
from the black robes
always at our elbows
patting our children on the heads
telling everyone
what to do
what did they know
of this great prairie
They did not love
the land
worked against it
from the words
in their black books

New words brought
to this open land
beautiful and dangerous
the fire swept the forest
the words said
you are mine

We would farm
but not as slaves
to those men brought from the east
who did not know us
who wanted only to sleep
with our women

The land was not always kind
but gave as it ebbed
We gave back, with thanks in sacrifice
while the whites
only wanted
They took lives without passion

How could they hang so many men
when they did not know
what I have seen
How could they cut into the river of life

Spring
in 83
he sent
the little packages
of tobacco
next year
the chiefs arrived
Big Bear
naked
chanted
prayed
To you who have given
what we have today
under
the painted
Thunderbird
the cloth offerings
he filled
the pipe
turning
east, north
west, south

prayed again
lit the bowl
it passed
from warrior to warrior
around the circle
incense
of sweetgrass
he prayed again
the Sun Dance began
men and women
dancers
thirsted
as prayer demanded
sacrifice
great deeds recounted
he danced
and made his promise

Yet angriest
my people
at Poundmaker's Sun dance
before the fighting
There were many there
who did not care
about the dance
They had left the hard life
on the plains
for a harder one
cattle in corrals
Craig the agent
was as stupid as Quinn
but luckier
there were 2000 then
the police who came
were lucky too
we went back out
to look for buffalo

The women
    kept us
        going
    making soup with mice
               snaring
        when we were at our worst
kept
    our spirits up
        singing
            collecting
        berries
    caring for crying
               children
        hunger
    soothing the angry
            washing
    skinning   delivering
tanning   mending
    sewing   protecting
        holding
            watching

We were hunting and
came too late
The Christian chiefs had signed
they were tired
weakened by words
We did not like the Company or Church
and were left out
made outlaws
Those whites calculating
kept the Cree apart
got to our Woodland brothers
who heard the Anglican voices
They would not wait for Piapot
many Cree felt the knife
the buffalo hunters out
unafraid to speak and
not heard
The gov't
won again
It was hard to watch
Beardy, Red Pheasant, Mistowasis
file off to the reserves
their white ministers in tow
you think the hunt is
everything
but written words stole
everything

And so Piapot
    in 84 walked among
  ashes
    scattering in the wind
   and bones
     his granddaughter dead from diarrhea
   and the old man's suicide
     with a stick he shoved
   down his own throat

     and then the fire
    swept through camp

      burning the trees
    where the dead
     had hung suspended

    from the ground
     skeletons scorched
   ominous
    portents
      black
       remains
        hanging

Isaac Cowie

      heard the stories from the edge
   of the hills

              saw the place later
    a whole campsite

            bleached
       by a torrential downpour
           of burning rain
        roaring thunder
              forked lightning
         doomed
              remains
                white bones
        forms when touched
               crumbled
                  to dust

a beautiful Cree maiden the sole survivor
        escaped by diving
          til she crossed the lake

Big Bear took them

        drew them

    through the hot and cold

        of prairie spring

    through the hell

        of swarming

   black flies

        mosquitoes

    eluding

        death in the land

    of his woodland

        brothers

    ancestors

        everywhere

    Then gave himself up

At night in dreams
the poplar leaves still
shimmer
and the white fluff floats
Last year's dried berries
dark red
in this dry spring
emaciated
But the walls so close
the bars so close
so little left to see
backed in and backed in
by then my eyes looked mostly inside

I came down from
Stony Mountain Pen
to Portage and Main
with a group of hunters
wearing old Pumas
this '85
but
no
one
noticed

By a high midday sun
   a pentacostal gull
      scouts the lake
         through a grainy dust
           like the still of '88

words
   now
   out
   of con
      text

Treaty 6 drew the lines

We return to the car and drive away

      smoke

          hanging

     under a
      greying

        sky

Cree Guides

*And he will teach them to smell history
in the wind, to touch it in stones polished
by the river, and to recognize its taste by
chewing certain herbs, without hurry as
one chews on sadness.*

Eduardo Galeano

Alan's 89 Jimmy's 78
Woodland Cree
trackers, trappers
hunters, fire fighters
men of the bush
take 'em
to the lakes
to look for
traces
      of old trading posts
burial grounds

     some day
tourists will
know
what was once
here before park
boundaries
drew lines

they are
the last
to know

Once they did work of wardens
now whitemen
have the high paying jobs
they
like to cook
for fire fighters
"just to be in the bush"
Jimmy says, the park doesn't call
him much anymore

    still knows
where pickerel and jack feed

        on all these lakes

Wear
layers
of things
and baseball hats
Jimmy's says
"SIMPLE GREEN"

On the way up
to burial site
of Alan's ancestors
Jimmy carefully
picks up five
round white stones
puts them in his pocket

Alan stands
next to a tree
he says was a sapling
just outside
the cabin door
where he was born
I take a picture
of him leaning on the trunk

Shows us
this place
at the Narrows
where a woman
was buried
alive
gone windigo

tells us
the story
of James Settee
who first came West
across the English River from the Bay
many years ago
James Settee
lined up
what he thought was
a moose
believed he'd brought
a curse on his people
when he found
he'd shot an animal
from the spirit-world
an animal he'd never seen before
a "red" deer – an elk – a waskesiu

Riley "Tiger" Bird
knows the island
in Crean
better than these guys
Tiger's 80 too
but Jimmy
says Tiger's too busy
chasing women
he looks at Alan
they both laugh
like hell
we'll need to make careful plans
to get him
out
this fall

They still drink
        HBC tea

    buy
        4 point blankets
        trousers
                from the company

            says Jimmy

Alan looks down at the fresh moose tracks

and Jimmy talks about
the place nearby
where he wounded
a bear
who returned
a year later
to destroy his tent
"bears are as smart
as people" Jimmy says

Watching out for

        places

protected

      from north winds

seeing

       calm

Copenhagen
    circle
    worn white
    onto back pockets

I read about their people
in the *Smithsonian Handbook of the North American Indian*

They read
sky   water   sun

at lunch
Jimmy says
whitemen
usually talk
about money
when resting   eating lunch
he says   Indians
talk about
women

and dreams

                    :

          of young woman
                    lightly
                              touching

               nuzzling
                                   under
             chin

he laughs hugely again

On the way
home
to Weyakwin
with a six pack of Blue
on his lap
Alan Nichols
carefully
looks back
for cops
each time
he takes a drink

      tracking

        hunted

          si (gh) tings

he keeps

      a glass

           (screw-top cap)

in his jacket pocket

    so he

         can

spit out

      snuff juice

      when

        he's

        in a

          car

eerie
how quietly
Jimmy and Alan
move through
bush
light
into the thickest growth
        hardly a sound

                magic
                        disappearances
                                outdoor
                silence

An Osprey

crowns

a tree

without

notice

d
   i
     v
       e
        s

fishes

a shallow

river

where

mallards parade

their colors

These boys

laugh

at questions

about Grey Owl

call him "Hoot Owl"

"Well you could tell

    knew he wasn't

        Indian

            just by the way he walked

                and 'cause he didn't wear socks"

                    says Jimmy

In 54

Jimmy saved
a language
professor's
five year old boy
lost
in the bush

park people gave up
sent for Jimmy

"Just headed into the bush
sat on a rock"
he said after he'd walked a few hours
"and imagined
where the boy might go"

found him before night fall

Jimmy laughs
            again
                  looks at me
      says
"You'll be translator when I get tired
                  then we'll know
                        what Alan's telling us"
                  laughs again

late afternoon

Crean's

       as smooth as glass

       glaring

blue and green

      blur

          everywhere

sandy beaches

             divide

     forest

       distance

heading home

     Jimmy

   tells of the timber wolves

       who still live

         'round the lake

       come out

        at night

On the Way to Waskesiu

to the memory of Jim Gibson and Ross Hutton

    I've got sand in my pants
    Puke in my shoes
    The Cleanin' Lady's
    Got the piss-pot Blues
    Swimmin' and surfin'
    In Murphy's Bay
    Well it looks like its gonna be another day.
            fragment from the "Waskesiu Song"
            by Ken Decker

The first stop
        Cloud 9 Wakaw
a few
        rounds
                playing
s h u f f l e b o a r d

word had it
the hotel
        t
            i
                l
                    t
                        e
                            d

s
    l
        a
            n
              t
                e
                  d
you could tell

p
u
c
k
s
f
e
l
l

o
f
f
s
a
m
e
s
i
d
e

86

old boys
                by the lake
                                thought
                        the whole town

                a
                n
                g
                led

Next stop
                by old route
St. Louis
                                Métis place
                drank
                                        on novelty
                                                balcony

Ni ck
al ready
ham mered
f alls
of f

second story

           o

              n

                t

                  o

                    ,

                        s

                            back

no pain
no damage

                        t

                s

        u   t

     j   o

             g   p

                            u

    l   u   h   n

      a   g   i   g

for another round

old boys there

call us long-hairs

    F A G S

in football jackets

      we get
          the
               hell
                     out
              fast
                          anyway

had to close one eye
by that time
to cross the narrow
train and highway
bridge north

On new route thru P.A.
       Wheezer and me

The old Beulah (black '56 Pontiac)

        w
                    e
        a
                    v
        e
                    s
        thru

        downtown

        RED

                        CHERRY

flashing

cop sees Wheezer get out
and take a shot of
asthma medicine but
       still tells Wheezer to
              walk the line
                     and touch
                        his
                              n
                                 o
                                    s
                              e

Wheezer can't do it he can hardly walk

Cop tells me to drive
takes beer in trunk but
we have beer in cooler in
apple box on front seat
that the cop doesn't look
in I drive on Wheezer
opens the box he got from
Safeway takes out two
apples Wheezer got a ticket
$52.50 now with me driving

     Car-i-van

The Star Fleet:

Gibber's	Black Bart
Ron Mutt's	Shaggon Waggon
Nick's	Mustang
Wilbur's	Dad's Car
Wheezer's	Beulah
My	Urinal

Last stop on the old route
        Mac Point
by now
    there were a couple
       too
        d
            r
                u
                    n
                       k

to get out

We never lasted long there

Insults
    the waitress fed up
    g
        o
           n
              e

On
    to the tent grounds
At the park
    pitched
              n

       e   t

    t   s
           nobody slept in

then off
       lookin' to get
whatever
    we could
       beg
       borrow or
       steal
s e a r c h i n g

    for
    next
    days
    parties

       Boy Scout
       Seven Mile
motor boats   beer for breakfast
    water damn cold
    good for the head
       throbbing
           with
"Old Nigger"   "Apple Jack"
           "Boh"

              watching the crazies chase
              pelicans
                         with boats
              forests nudging up to lake

"Old Nigger" always
          drunk with bag on
wisdom was
          you'd be fine
if you couldn't see
          what you were drinking

          hootch
porch climber

Stories
                              Beginnings

When the rain comes
they run and hide their heads
They might as well be dead

　　When the rain comes
　　When the rain comes

Ra – a – a – a – a – a – ain
　　　I don't mind

Shi – i – i – i – i – i – i – ne
　　　weather's fine

Star Fleet   v   Stilletoes
(Eastsiders)   (Westsiders)

high noon

blurred

game

ended

when

I

became

first base

just after

a line drive

I couldn't see

hit the glove

my final out

Nailed
      for drinking in
           "other than a dwelling"
               they called it

Screwdrivers

          When
the cop found me
early in the morning
wrapped in an old blanket
drinking
from a lemonade tin

hauled down to the cells
             booked
(told him he looked like Dano)
lucky
to get
     away

Three days later: Sunday

     wrung out dish rags
"Skinny" red as a lobster
lost his glasses
turning his head for the moose
we suckered him to look for

a few beer left for the trip home
sick from non-stop drinking
Car rolled
       in the ditch
  killed
       two guys
from Holy Cross
made no impression

Usually we stopped for a burger
      or something
         on the way
           home
Well there was this one time
we went
     into the restaurant
       in Wakaw
There was a bunch of us
Gibber, Wheezer, Me, Nick, Sheep, Black Molly
Wilbur, Doc, Hound Dog, Rocky, Duck

First
we all ordered
a regular full meal
Then
Gibber said he was
still hungry
So
we called over
Chinese owner
And
all ordered another
full meal

fish and chips
spaghetti
chops
chinese food

stuff like that

Then
we ordered
dessert
which they
could hardly believe

Gibber started
playing the piano
in the corner

And
the guy brought
his family
to the kitchen door

Finally
        the guy started
                bringing out
                        old stale
                        cinnamon buns
                                and donuts
                                        for us to eat

"Free"
        he said
                and we ate
                        them all

Guy's
        family still
                staring
                        at us
                                as we

Paid
        we all had
                lotsa money
                        back then

We laughed
about that one
as we rolled home

Back to jobs, school
        and stuff like that

Well it looks like its gonna be another day
      hey hey
Things usually seem to turn out that way
      hey hey
Waitin' for the angels to come and take me away
      hey hey
Well it looks like its gonna be another day.

    K. Decker

Washington 1992

around this city

       streets of the states

   monuments

    horses

    heroes

     of war

Black drummers drum in the bottom of old white discarded plastic pails

Gulls swarm

        the Lincoln monument

      the Vietnam monument

        no Martin Luther King

     the slow start/
              into the depth of the war

            the narrow end

Black drummers drum on the bottom of old white discarded plastic pails

     a thick book of names

        all the tears

        all the poems

      flowers

     this public display

            agony

        memories of life and death

Black drummers drum on the bottom of old white discarded plastic pails

        this terrible
              war
          still has no context here
            among the lost
                the homeless
            the confusion

        this city
              hard
                  to walk around
            the poor   the homeless
               small villages
                    of black men
                          under tarpaulin
                  veterans

        this plastic
            homes
          plastic homes
              homes on the edge
                  of the White House
            in the heart of the capital

Black drummers drum on the bottom of old white discarded plastic pails

    this city

        of fog and rain
              overcast
        drizzle
           can't get thru the plastic tents
             protect

Black drummers drum on the bottom of old white discarded plastic pails

    slavery

  academics
        study to understand

    a privilege

      to explain

a poem left

        for a father

                under a name

  you see yourself

      in the dark reflection

    of stone

hard

    for a Canadian

   to fathom

      all this war

      all this freedom

Black drummers drum on the bottom of old white discarded plastic pails

      understanding

        slavery

       huge war memorials

walking away

                dark and shining stone

        lower than the exuberance

                       of past centuries

                          celebrations

            glory

                valour

       Vets

            wearing rings of bullets

a young boy asks

            his mother
             :
       who won the war?

and after a long silence

                  and no response

            he asks again

       who won that war, Mom?

his Mom says

         "that's a good question"

Mickeyapolis

Words of course are the most
important drug of mankind.
                    Rudyard Kipling

is a white
                    city
        filled
with the latest
                    architecture
        geometrical
                            even pastel

the graffiti says:

        God or Money

the blacks clean
                    this city
        polish
                the windows
in the great
                    clean
        modern high
                    rises
they don't seem to be
                    in/of
                            this place

it is not their place

                    out
                            of place

white teachers
        watch over

take care
care take
      the black children
           in the park
   across
      from the
      Walker Art Centre
where we see

      the latest

   outdoor sculpture gardens

next to a road
      built by
   mostly white
        workers

but back downtown
      the blacks

           are still

   waiting on the whites

Words
          of course are
                    the most important
                              drug
                                        of mankind
                                                  R.K.

But
          billboard shows:

                    Kahlua

                              in coffee next to a chocolate baby

(it tugs at
                    those at home
                                        surrounded)

At night
          Blacks play
                    jazz in the clubs

Here
          on most billboards
                              white sex
                                        sells everything

Billboard shows
                    white sex
                              sells
                                        everything

We come here to take it all in
        but its hard to get in
                not everyone gets in

Lutheran Brotherhood
        owns one of the most
                glorious steel and glass
                        buildings in the downtown

and of course Shows

TV shows
        Ellis Island
                rags to riches dream
                      come true

Cartoon shows
                violence

Street shows
        blonde blue-eyed white
                men in grey pin-striped suit

News shows
        the jack-booted
                skin-heads

Strip shows
        on Hennipen

No shows
        on Sunday

Late show
        Johnny

Money show
                afternoon

Movie shows
                Batman

show show show

all

                for

                                show

                downtown

all is

                                for show

they know how to show

Most stuff

                        is cheaper

                health

        costs

                        not all

        can

                pay

Calvin Griffiths liked it plain and simple

I like

the new baseball

blacks

once watched

from sidelines

it's a clean show
                    downtown

a good show
a good clean show
a good clean white show

carefully painted white for show

showed for shine
sparkling silver show
a trendy pastel show
a dandy show

on show for some

Black T-shirts
                    say funny things

"North"

"Member Alcatraz Swim Team"

Mostly I think
of the Frank Lloyd Wright houses
wanted to break
down the barrier
between inside and
out

Rauschenberg's art (in the Walker)
        destroyed the privileged
             viewer

but it means nothing here

where there is so much
        cleaning done

cleaners downtown
        are everywhere
            every day

dirt
        is worked
              away

and the cleaners go
          away
    at night

clean as a
      Swiss
    city

movements fine

     regulated

      standardized

Mary

        thinking of Disney

    calls it

             Mickeyapolis

the myth lives here
           Paul Bunyan
      history for the books
        history for the birds

heritage preservation
      is slowly failing
        slowly the decaying
          old buildings gradually
         falling
            into disuse
              in this enormously
                 wealthy
                    city

the once grand old Leamington
        will soon
          be gone

will soon
     disappear

   implosion

          the bartender

    hopes

show piece
show girl
show trial
show down

Windcatcher: Bringing the Inside/Out
after Mike Olito's sculpture

Between the realms there once stretched a huge
and seeming emptiness; this was Ginnungagap.
The rivers that sprang from Hvergelmir streamed into the
void. The yeasty venom in them thickened and congealed
like slag, and the rivers turned into ice. That venom
also spat out drizzle – an unending dismal hagger that,
as soon as it settled, turned into rime. So it went on
until all the northern part of Ginnungagap was heavy
with layers of ice and hoar frost, a desolate place haunted
by gusts and skuthers of wind.

Edda

The Windcatcher is
                    inside
where it
                    turns
                                    when Mary
                        pulls
            on its black tail

deer skull
        white Norse
                crown

we keep it in
        can't do
            much
                here

Needs
        wind
     to return

          to spin
        to play with it
        bring out the red

Make
        it part of
            things bigger
         than itself

Outside
        at night
            the wind builds
                  and tears
            cloth
      chain
          rattles
        as the white
                  Aesir horses
              swoop down
        to lift it away
             with them
light brown stones weight it down
             keep it here

Darkness
                    comes
          shifts
                    Loki in the wind
                              waves
                    its tail
                              (that mostly hangs
                                                  still
                              here in the living room
                                        wears
                                             little)

Indoor
                    air
                              barely
                                             moves
          when someone passes
                                             stands
                              protected
                    death
                                   black
          only stirs
                    plays lightly on wooden
                                             chimes

Rushes
                    out of stillness
          bringing
                              cloth
                    sticks
               chain
bone   stone
                                  suddenly
          into motion

          feathers bristle
       looking from
                                        inside
   it haunts this city neighborhood
                  where wind is hard to see
                  (they must think we're Druids)
   Await the warm
                           winds
                  or Njord
                       to weave new patterns
                              with cloth

                                              scarecrows wear
       His winds   calm
                                  wild fires
                  save crops

Exposure

Sanctuary

Art

Wood

Changes

Weather

"For Fear of Divine Retribution"

in the place where the "Land Gets Broken"
for Elsie Koochicum and Valerie Rider

Here in the land the Creator gave them
Man – Who – Took – the – Coat
told the Queen's men five times
that he would not leave
this place where the sacred grasses grew
grasses dried and mixed with tobacco
blessed by the holy men
smoked in ceremonies
that sealed the great treaty
a place for the Assiniboine people
sacred to the Assiniboine people

Here "Where the Land Becomes Broken"
where the Creator
gave so much —
the hawk, antelope
the tall thin trees for
dog travois and lodge poles
wild hops, turnip
choke cherries, rose buds
bull berries, goose berries
currants, wild rhubarb
      eaten fresh or dried
soothing winds peaceful lakes
      high calming panoramas
where in solitude
renewal came
with fasting through visions

the first thunder
spirit of the Sun Dance
ceremonies
where the sacred grasses
came alive with fire
in the stone pipe bowls
to wake up the grandfather spirits
who watched over us

Five times he told them
but each time the Queen's men
came back to tell them
that they had to move
from the great land
this land they knew for so long —

"They listened to my proposal
and all the reasons I gave
why the government thought
it better for them to move
from here. They promised
to answer me in a day or
two. Two days later they all
turned up again and each
made a speech and they all
agreed in this that they wanted
to remain in this section of
the country and settle permanently
on Maple Creek Reserve. Their
chief arguments against moving
were that they were brought
up in this country, that although
they had given up their country
to the Queen who had promised
them a Reserve in whatever
part of the country they
liked to pick out that they
did not like the northern
country or the Indians living
there and hoped the Government
would allow them to remain
here. The-Man-Who-Took-the-Coat
asked me to tell you that this

was the first time he had ever refused to do as
the Queen asked him, but he said he loved the country
and wanted to remain here
and hoped the government
would not be angry with him."
    Indian Agent McIllree, 1882

The farm instructor
had already told them
how good the crops could be
and the potatoes grew
and the hay was good

Man-Who-Took-the-Coat
told them he could
not break his promise
made in the presence
of the grandfather spirits
who awoke with the smoke
from the pipes
spirits who would avenge
those who made sacred
vows as they watched and listened
— fire lightning thunder and floods —
would haunt those who broke
the solemn oaths to the powerful
spirits that watch over these hills

The government men had changed their minds
now wanted no tribes to settle in the hills
the government broke their own solemn promises
they had promised the bounty and benevolence of the Queen

And when they would not go
the government began to starve the Assiniboine
gave them salt pork
that made them sick and weak
     — salt pork to a people used
     to fresh meat
     nausea, vomiting and
     diarrhea followed the sick
     and dying

The government tells them they
have a new home
The government tells them they

                      must go

the government begins
the forced removal

in dreams she remembered
The walk the long journey
on foot
began on a railway flatcar
that overturned killing and
injuring many people
They had to walk to Maple Creek
to where the railway was to take them
at Maple Creek where
Mounties forced them
onto the flatcars

after the accident
we refused to get back on
the flatcars
we walked with police escort for weeks until we reached
the Qu'Appelle
they put us in a place
where many Cree had died

"the Skull Mountanettes"
where an epidemic had
killed the Cree
a smallpox epidemic
a place haunted by the spirits
of the crying and the lame

at night I hear
the wailing at night I
heard the cry of the hawk and eagle
return to visit this sad place
soaked in tears

we did not want this land
        where the Cree were buried
we longed for the hills
        the place of our ancestors
we longed for the smell and
        taste of our grasses
we longed for the sound
        of our drums and the
                echo from the hills
we longed for the place
        where our dances came from

some went back to starve
some go back in dreams

The police surgeon wrote to
tell Macdonald that many
would die that the salt pork
could not be digested by weak
and starving people who
were used to fresh meat.

Man-Who-Took-the-Coat
told them / told them
many times that he could
not leave that the hills
of his chosen homeland
where the great elders
lay high on the hills
high where the men fasted
high where the eagles turned
high in the blue solitude
high where the thin grey line
woke the spirits in the skies

Wazi-ka the place where
the land gets broken

Wazi-ka the place where
babies were washed

Wazi-ka the place where
the elders watch

Man-Who-Took-the-Coat told
them it was the first
time he had ever refused
the Queen and that
he was sorry to do so

Dewdney hoped that:
  "starvation would drive them
  from the Fort Walsh area"

Dewdney said that
  the "hunger crisis" made
  the move necessary

Dewdney created
  the "hunger crisis"

Dewdney lied
  to the Assiniboine

Dewdney betrayed
  a desperate starving people

how many ways do you explain
                    removal

how many ways are there to explain

          forced removal

              starvation

how do you explain this to children
                    today

all these scars
          accumulated

the elders believe the train crash
              was planned

the derailment deliberate

they felt they were herded
          onto the train like cattle

the reserve here
of Carry-the-Kettle is much smaller
there has been so much suffering here
in a hundred years the wounds
    have not healed
so many lives taken
so much life denied

and yet Sintaluta (the red fox)
visits and in the song
the medicine man sings
he prays for the fox to return
with something for the young
at the end of the day

The Garden Party

A play

Jimmie Chinn and Hazel Wyld

Samuel French — London
New York - Toronto - Hollywood

THE GARDEN PARTY

First presented at Hampton Hill Playhouse on 12th June, 1999 with the following cast:

Jan	Patricia Bottomley
Richard	Michael Godley
Hettie	Heather Couper
Eunice	Rosemary Oliver
Miles	Gareth Parsons
Sam	Susan Reoch
Charlie	David Hannigan
Ben	David Wheatley
Brice	Peter Slater

Directed by Jimmie Chinn
Designed by Gordon Edwards
Lighting by Chris Davies
Sound by Charles Halford and Peter Cook

CHARACTERS

Jan
Richard, her husband
Hettie, her sister-in-law
Eunice, her neighbour
Miles, her grandson
Sam, her daughter
Charlie, her younger son
Ben, her elder son
Brice, a stranger

The action of the play takes place in the garden of an old house on the Isle of Wight on a day in summer

Time—the present

For Andrew

ACT I

The garden and patio of an old house which overlooks the sea on the Isle of Wight. A summer morning

The house is R, *with french windows opening from it on to a patio; from the patio a back gate in the high wall leads down to the beach. There are shrubs; plants, including an agapanthus; hanging baskets etc.; and several items of garden furniture, none of them modern or new: a long wooden table with a bench either side and a chair at each end, a lounger, a smaller table and several other chairs, all in wicker-work. A watering can and a local newspaper are in evidence*

When the play begins, there is brilliant sunshine and the distant sound of the sea and seagulls. (These sounds continue throughout the play)

Richard, a battered Panama on his head, is half asleep on the lounger, a copy of "The Times" crossword on his lap. Further off sits Hettie, reading a book and with a large hat shading her from the sun

After a while, Jan comes out of the house, dressed informally in shorts and a baggy T-shirt. She is carrying a tablecloth and a jug of flowers which she places on the long table

Jan Haven't you gone?
Hettie Sorry...?
Jan I'm talking to Richard. He hasn't gone yet.
Hettie Are you surprised? He's fast asleep.
Richard (*from beneath his Panama*) I am not asleep. I was just resting my eyes.
Hettie And snoring.
Jan And have you been for your walk? Taken your exercise? No.
Richard (*going back to his crossword*) I can't keep walking. And where am I supposed to walk to?
Jan (*watering plants on the terrace*) You have your contraption in the bedroom. It cost a fortune. Walk on that.
Richard After lunch, eh? Always more beneficial after lunch.
Jan Isn't it time you set out for the ferry?
Richard Plenty of time. It's a five-minute run; five minutes there, five minutes back.

Jan Nine-and-a-half minutes, dear. I've timed it. Often.
Richard (*without moving*) If you say so.
Hettie Anything I can do?
Jan Not yet, dear. Later maybe.
Hettie I've got that pain again. Top of my legs, bottom of my spine.
Richard Creeping paralysis, dear — bound to be.
Hettie That's right — make fun. Of course if my bedroom wasn't quite so damp ...

No response

> Last night's rain came in again. Drip, drip, drip. Is it any wonder I'm always so tired?

Jan (*trying not to listen to any of this*) We'll try to get it done before the winter sets in. (*Pointedly*) Won't we, Richard?
Richard (*about the crossword*) "Individual effort by Scotsman — a wise fellow!" Any ideas, Hettie?
Hettie How many letters ...?

From off stage we hear Eunice approaching the back gate, singing "Happy Birthday" to Richard. She enters, carrying a box with a cake in it, and moves to Richard

Hettie (*obviously not over-fond of Eunice*) Oh, God!
Eunice (*kissing Richard on the cheek*) Who's the birthday boy, then?
Richard Eunice! How sweet. What is it?
Eunice Your cake.
Richard (*lifting the box lid and peering inside*) Really! How very kind. Magnificent. I adore cake. Cake is my passion. Now, if I had a wife who could bake cakes ... (*He puts his hand in the box as if to try a bit*)
Eunice (*slapping Richard's wrist*) Ah, naughty! You'll spoil it. Morning, Hettie. (*Sarcastically*) How's the ankle?

Detecting the sarcasm, Hettie ignores Eunice and returns to her book

Jan (*looking into the box*) Eunice — it's beautiful. You are clever. He's quite right of course, I'm a lousy cake-maker.
Richard On the other hand, she makes a superb roast and the best chips you've ever tasted.
Jan Not a great asset at a birthday party.
Hettie And I'm good for nothing, I suppose.

Eunice, Richard and Jan exchange glances

Eunice Now, how about a nice glass of Pimms before the others arrive?
Richard Splendid idea.

Hettie Not for me, thank you.
Eunice I'll see to it. Where do you want this?
Jan Hide it. I want to bring it out as a surprise.

Eunice exits into the house, taking the cake

Richard What surprise? I've just seen it.
Jan Not you — the children.
Richard Ah, I see — the children.
Jan Who are probably, at this moment, straining their eyes, peering from the boat vainly looking for a friendly fatherly face waiting to greet them at the quayside.
Richard What about the Pimms? We can't disappoint Eunice.
Jan When you get back. You're driving. What if you get breathalysed?
Richard On one glass of Pimms ... Come on.
Jan Richard ... !
Richard Anyway, if I am arrested I shall tell them that today is my seventieth birthday and that I needed a drink because it's very depressing to be seventy.
Jan (*going back to watering plants*) Just admit it: you hate birthdays.
Richard Only my own.
Jan I can recall you being just as depressed when you were sixty.
Richard But at least I was working — at least I was *doing* something.
Jan Rubbish. You hated being forty — and fifty. I expect you were just as miserable when you were born. Isn't that right, Hettie?
Hettie If you're both talking nonsense now, I can't imagine what you'll be like when you're drunk!

Eunice enters bearing a tray with a jug, Pimms, lemonade, ice, fruit and glasses etc. on it

Eunice Oh, lovely — are we all going to get roaring drunk before the party? Hettie?
Hettie (*rising*) I'm going indoors. This sun is far too hot already.

Hettie exits into the house

Eunice puts the tray on the table and begins to prepare the drinks

Richard (*mock-pleading*) Perhaps just a tiny one — please!
Jan No, no, no, Richard: when you get back from the ferry!
Richard (*rising*) OK ... OK ... No need to nag.
Jan You're not going out in that hat, surely?
Richard I most certainly am. I don't want sunstroke. (*He walks* DS, *looking out at the "view"*) It's going to be a scorcher. I shall take my grandchildren round the rock pools when the tide goes out.

Jan Can you hear all this, Eunice? (*To Richard*) You never listen to a word I say, do you? The grandchildren aren't coming — just Ben and Charlie and Sam.

Richard I don't remember you telling me that.

Jan Oh, Richard — stop pretending to be senile. This is a family day, a special day; I wanted just us. Not Kay, not Tim, and no grandchildren. Just the five of us. And Hettie of course.

Richard I see.

Jan (*moving to Richard, gentler now*) It'll be like the old days. I thought you'd like that. Turn the clock back a little. Anyway, you know how wearing the kids can be.

Richard Who's looking after the boy then?

Jan Well, Tim must. That's his job.

Richard gives Jan a look

All right, Sam *might* have to bring him. Now go.

Richard Won't Kay and Tim feel left out? They'll think we don't see them as family.

Jan Everybody understood. Anyway, they aren't family — they're in-laws.

Richard Blowed if I understand. Still, as long as you're happy. (*He kisses the top of Jan's head*)

Jan looks at her watch

All right, all right, I'm going.

Jan I never said a word.

Eunice (*stirring the Pimms concoction*) Here we are — nearly ready.

Richard (*kissing Eunice on the cheek*) Don't drink it all before I get back. Got to go — I'm under starter's orders. (*To Jan*) Car keys?

Jan In the hall, dear — where they always are.

Richard Of course.

Richard exits into the house

Jan, almost at screaming pitch, makes a gesture of impatience

Eunice (*laughing*) Come on — have a drink. (*She pours two glasses of Pimms*)

Jan I'm sorry — did I snap at him? He knows I can't bear unpunctuality.

Eunice Stop fussing.

Jan (*taking a glass*) He's beginning to be such hard work. And if I do invite the grandchildren they wear him out. He's not a young man any more.

Eunice And you're not that old — is that what you mean?

Jan No, Eunice — that is *not* what I mean.

Eunice I'm only teasing; come on, lighten up. Cheers.

Jan Cheers. (*She sits at the table*)

Eunice Are you all right?

Jan Fine. Hettie's playing up again; Richard refuses to take his exercise ...

Eunice You mustn't treat him like an invalid; he hates it.

Jan He had a heart attack, Eunice. Scared us all to death. What if it happens again?

Eunice I've told you: you worry too much. Just look at him — he's adorable.

Jan I know, so you keep telling me. I just don't want to lose him. What would I do?

Eunice Now stop it. At least you've had the perfect marriage. Look at me: three husbands and all of them a dead loss.

Jan You were unlucky, that's all.

Eunice Unlucky! You can say that again.

Jan Anyway, Sebastian was all right: you told me so.

Eunice Sebastian? He was number four, dear. And I only lived with him.

Jan Oh, God — I lose track of them all.

Eunice He was the best looking, definitely. Adonis, my dear. Fantastic sex.

Jan So what went wrong there?

Eunice He couldn't see the point of keeping that lovely body all for one woman when there were so many out there who'd be grateful. Plus he was costing me a fortune.

Jan So you asked him to leave.

Eunice I threw him out — yes.

Jan (*laughing*) I never know when to believe you. Is all this true?

Eunice Gospel. You see, you know nothing, woman. Look at you: you have it all; a devoted husband, adoring children, gorgeous grandchildren, a contented life ...

Jan Practically no money to live on for the past four years ...

Eunice Oh, come on — money isn't everything. Richard made an error of judgement — that's all. You mustn't hold it against him.

Jan I don't. I just wish it wasn't such a struggle to make ends meet. We have Hettie now; remember?

Eunice She's no trouble, is she ... I mean — really?

Jan I suppose not. Life did change just a tiny bit when she arrived, though.

Eunice How's the ...? (*She makes a gesture indicating "drink"*)

Jan We simply pretend it doesn't happen. So does she.

Eunice Well, forget it all — just enjoy the day. You do realize this will be the first time I've met your children?

Jan I hope you're in for a treat.

Eunice I've lived here ... What is it? Six months? How come I've never seen them?

Jan (*rising, moving away; evasively*) Oh, I don't know — they just haven't
been down since Richard's illness. They all lead such busy lives: Charlie
works at the airport so he's on shifts, and Sam ... Well, most of her time is
taken up with her son. (*She tries to change the subject*) Anyway, they're
far too busy to want to come and see us. (*She sits*)

Eunice You've missed one out. Ben. Rich, good looking *and* unmarried.

Jan Hands off. You're much too old for Ben. And he's far too interested in
making money to have time for girlfriends.

Eunice Well, I can't wait to meet them. Another Pimms?

Jan Good heavens, no. One's enough for me.

Eunice Shouldn't you be getting changed?

Jan Oh, no. It wouldn't be me if I dressed up.

Eunice You're not telling me that ensemble is it?

Jan I haven't got glad rags like you, Eunice.

Eunice Then I shall lend you something.

Jan Don't be silly.

Eunice Rubbish, it's no problem. This is a very special occasion and I'm
going to take you in hand. Look at your hair; we can do something with that.

Jan (*embarrassed*) Eunice, stop it.

Eunice You've gorgeous eyes and you don't make enough of them.

Jan Please don't fuss, I'm fine as I am.

Eunice (*refilling her glass*) If you say so. I could always slip away after the
introductions.

Jan No way. I need you here. Besides, you've helped with all the food. Don't
go, please.

Something unspoken seems to hang in the air

Eunice You are funny. I hope Richard's looking forward to this party more
than you seem to be.

Jan I am. Honestly. Anyway, it isn't my party—it's for him. He loves having
them here.

Eunice He must have been a wonderful father: kind, patient.

Jan He was. Still is. He used to miss them like crazy when he was working
away.

Eunice Months on end, you said.

Jan Yes, but he always made up for it when he came home. And, when we
could, school holidays particularly, we went on location with him.

Eunice He was obviously in great demand.

Jan Yes, but he was one of the top lighting-cameramen in the country. In the
world maybe.

Eunice What about his collection? Has he missed it yet?

Jan Oh, Eunice — don't spoil everything.

Eunice You'll have to tell him sooner or later.

Jan (*getting up; on edge*) I will. I promise. But not today. Tomorrow perhaps — after the party. Now, change the subject, please.

Eunice (*tactfully, as always*) Look, I'm going home to slip into something cooler.

Jan Yes, and I must get a move on.

Eunice Are you sure I can't look out something stunning for you while I'm at it?

Jan Oh, why the hell not? But nothing too saucy. Nothing with a slit up the front.

Eunice (*delighted*) And your hair? A touch of make-up?

Jan Go on. But remember, they forecast a storm for later on.

Eunice Rubbish — there's not a cloud in the sky.

Jan Oh, yes, there is. (*She points out front*) A tiny one, just there — see?

Hettie comes out of the house

Hettie Any sign of them yet? Let's hope the ferry's on time — you know how Richard hates to wait.

Eunice (*heading to the back gate*) I'll be right back. You're going to look fantastic!

Eunice exits

Hettie (*sitting*) Wretched woman. What in my day used to be called a "party-girl".

Jan She's a good friend.

Hettie (*looking at the local paper*) Need any help? I'm more than willing.

Jan (*putting the cloth on the table*) No — I shall be fine.

Hettie I didn't get Richard a present. I mean, what do you buy the man who has everything?

Jan gives her a look

Some of these prices — who can afford them? A simple two-up, two-down here and they're asking a king's ransom. And the flats are all so poky.

Jan (*busy*) Oh, come along — you wouldn't be happy living alone.

Hettie I don't know why you always say that. When Samuel died I was perfectly content to live alone.

Jan Do you think I should move this agapanthus into the shade? (*She carries the plant over into the shade*)

Hettie I was devastated, yes, but it didn't mean I wanted to be surrounded by hoards of people.

Jan (*about the plant*) There we are — that's better.

Hettie Besides, if anything were to happen to Richard you wouldn't want me under your feet.

Jan If anything happened to Richard, Hettie, I wouldn't be able to afford to live here. Anyway, nothing *is* going to happen to him. (*She heads for the door into the house*) Right — I'd best get on. You'll give me a call if they come in the back way.

Jan exits into the house

Hettie, left alone, goes over to the table and takes a sip of Pimms from a glass. She savours it, quite likes the taste and takes another mouthful

A football suddenly appears over the back wall and rolls past Hettie: she picks it up, annoyed

Hettie Damn kids! (*Calling*) You're not getting it back! This is private property and you've no right to ——

A boy, Miles, appears at the gate. He is dressed in shorts and a T-shirt which make him appear younger than he probably is. He stops dead and looks across at Hettie, an odd, vacant look in his eyes

(*Kindly*) Good heavens! Is it you? Can it really be you? Miles? My, how you've grown. You remember me, surely. I'm Hettie, dear. Your grand-pa's sister. Is this your ball? Come on then — come and get it.

Miles doesn't move. He seems slightly nervous of Hettie, unsure what to do next

Don't be silly — I'm not going to hurt you.

Sam appears at the gate, hot and sticky from her journey. She is carrying a bag

Sam Hallo, Hettie. You're not expecting him to fetch that, I hope? He's not a dog. (*To Miles*) You're not being a nuisance to Hettie, are you?

Hettie throws the ball to Miles. It lands at his feet where he leaves it for the moment

God, it's so hot. We're not eating out here, surely? Is there a cold drink? I'm exhausted.

Hettie There's some sort of concoction in that jug but it must be warm by now. How was your journey?

Sam (*sitting at the table and removing her shoes*) Not bad. At least the ferry was on time. But the tourists! Hundreds of them. I swore last time I'd never come across here in the summer again. Can I have some of this?

Hettie (*sitting again, not happy in company*) Help yourself.

Sam (*pouring a drink; to Miles*) Come in, darling. Don't just stand there.

Miles picks up his ball, moves further off and sits

It didn't work out then, Hettie?

Hettie I'm sorry?

Sam The house. Weren't you thinking of moving back to the mainland? Didn't care too much for the island you said.

Hettie It's a question of finding the right ——

Sam God, this tastes good. It's ages since I've had Pimms. Where's Mum and Dad?

Hettie Didn't Richard pick you up?

Sam Oh, no. Don't tell me he's gone down there to meet us? I told him Charlie was bringing the car across. What the hell's the matter with him?

Charlie enters through the back gate, wiping his hands on a hanky

Charlie Those bloody garage doors! Dad still hasn't mended them. What does he *do* all day? Look, I've cut myself on that rusty lock.

Sam (*drinking, unconcerned*) Guess what?

Charlie Don't tell me. Not trouble already.

Sam Dad's gone down to fetch us.

Charlie I thought you said ——

Sam Don't get angry; it's far too hot.

Charlie What's that stuff?

Sam Life on the Island, dear — Pimms.

Charlie I'll have to have a shower; I can't sit around like this all day.

Sam I told you to bring some shorts, but, oh no.

Charlie I'm not Ben. I haven't got Ben's legs for a start. I can't go poncing around in shorts, topless with a gold chain!

Sam Who's going to tell them?

Charlie I couldn't care less who tells them. It's not my problem.

Sam indicates to Charlie, by look or gesture, not to ignore Hettie, who is looking ill at ease

Oh, hallo, Hettie. I thought you'd gone.

Hettie I would have thought it was quite obvious that I haven't "gone" as you call it.

Sam Weren't you going to buy a house in Worthing or somewhere?

Hettie I became quite ill. Run down. My brother insisted I stay.

Charlie I see. Look, I must have a drink. (*Calling loudly into the house*) Mum — is there a cold beer or something...?

Sam I hope Dad doesn't insist we all go down to the beach. They'll be swarming down there today. Did you get the presents?

Charlie Left them in the car till later. (*Calling again*) Mum! Get your arse out here!

Jan (*off, calling, excited*) Charlie ... Charlie, is that you ...?

Jan appears from the house, an apron tied round her waist, a lettuce in her hand. She is almost girlish with excitement at seeing her visitors

I had no idea you were here. Hettie, why didn't you tell me?

Jan throws herself into Charlie's arms and kisses him

Hettie (*feeling in the way*) I think I'll go to my room for a while; it really is too hot for me out here.

Hettie goes off indoors

Jan (*throwing her arms around Sam*) My darlings! I'm so happy to see you.

Charlie I'm in dire need of alcoholic refreshment and I don't mean poncy Pimms!

Jan You know where the fridge is.

Charlie exits into the house

(*Seeing Miles and rushing over to him*) And you *have* brought him! Miles — my lovely, lovely Miles! (*She throws her arms around him*)

Miles, unhappy with all this fuss, stands rigid and doesn't respond

Sam Leave him, Mother; he gets embarrassed by all that.

Jan He's never too old for his nan's affection. What happened?

Sam I had to bring him. Tim had a "meeting".

Jan You do surprise me. Eleventh hour, of course.

Sam Not now, please. Anyway, I'm beginning not to care. Who needs him?

Jan Obviously you do or you wouldn't still be there.

Sam Don't start all that now. Besides, where would I go?

Jan You could come here. Miles would love it, wouldn't you?
Sam Don't make me laugh. You and me under the same roof. We'd strangle each other within a week.
Jan Dad found you all right?
Sam No. We must have passed him. I rang in the week — told him we'd be fetching the car over. What's the matter with him?
Jan He forgets. Don't worry. He'll go mad, hanging around down there in this heat.

Charlie enters from the house, a can of beer in his hand

Charlie What've you done to the den? You've changed it.
Jan I've decorated it — that's all.
Charlie *You* have?
Jan And why not? Your dad went out for the day and Hettie stood by and criticized.
Charlie Looks a bit bare, doesn't it? What happened to ... ?

There is a moment of awkward silence

Jan Where's Ben?
Charlie *(sitting)* Here we go. What did I tell you, Sam?
Sam I'm keeping out of it. Can I have some more of this? *(She helps herself to more drink).*
Jan Come on, tell me the worst. Where is he?
Charlie Dead for all we know.
Jan Charles! Don't say that. Not even in jest. Now where is he? What's happened?
Charlie He knew the arrangements. Eleven at Lymington for the eleven-fifteen ferry. He didn't show.
Jan But he promised he'd be here!
Charlie If you haven't learned what Ben's promises are by now ... He promised me something once, if I remember.
Jan Oh, don't let's have all that today for heaven's sake. This has got to be a nice day. A nice, nice day — right?
Sam It will be, Mum. Stop fussing. You know, I've rather taken to this. *(She drinks)*
Jan Eunice will be back in a minute — she'll make some more.
Charlie ⎱ *(together)* Eunice ...?
Sam ⎰
Sam Not another of your waifs and strays.
Jan Eunice is my new neighbour. *(She lowers her voice)* And please be kind to Hettie.

Charlie We are kind to Hettie. We're always kind to Hettie. What did I say, Sam, on the way over? "Let's all be kind to Hettie!"

Jan (*hitting Charlie playfully*) Stop it! I want no trouble, Charlie, no trouble at all.

Charlie How can there be? Ben's not here.

Jan Surely he'd have phoned if anything had happened. He's got a phone, hasn't he?

Charlie Several, knowing him. A mobile in every suit, a fax in the car, and a modem stuck up his arse.

Jan Charlie! I mean it!

Eunice enters through the back gate. She has changed her dress and carries a fruit flan in one hand, a can of hair spray and a dress for Jan in the other

Eunice (*with a flourish*) I am come bearing gifts for the birthday table: a strawberry flan, a frock, a can of hair-spray and thou, my love!

Charlie (*to himself*) Oh, God! Another bloody weirdo!

Eunice I am Eunice Next-Door, as your mother prefers to call me. It saves her trying to remember my surnames, of which I have many. Now, don't tell me — you must be Sam. (*She puts the flan on the table and shakes Sam's hand*)

Sam That's me.

Eunice And you — please don't get up — must be Charlie.

Charlie You mean not good-looking enough for Ben.

Eunice I meant no such thing. Naughty boy. I know your type — fishing for compliments.

Jan No, he just can't resist a dig.

Charlie Ben is, as I'm sure you've gathered, Mother's little soldier. Her pet lamb.

Eunice Really. No, that isn't the impression I got.

Jan Don't encourage him, Eunice. He's going for the sympathy vote. Poor little unloved Charlie.

Charlie I didn't say I was unloved. We were all loved. Ben just had the edge.

Sam What he means, Eunice, is that Ben has ended up very rich and successful and that, not unnaturally, it pisses us off.

Jan The silly thing is, Charlie is just as successful in a different way. He has a sweet wife — Kay — three gorgeous children: Louise who is ——

The following is obviously a ritual for Jan and Charlie

Charlie Twelve ...

Jan Jack who is ——

Charlie Seven ...
Jan And Christopher, who is five. Right?
Charlie Right, Mother — except Christopher's called Stephen.
Jan Well, if perhaps I saw them more often ...!
Eunice (*going to Miles, arms outstretched*) And who is *this* handsome young
man?

Miles turns away, alarmed by this stranger

Sam He's my son, Eunice — and he's shy.
Eunice Don't tell me. I know how he feels. I've been a martyr to shyness all
my life. (*To Jan*) Come along, you: make-over time.
Jan Oh dear — must I?
Eunice Sam, will you tell your mother, I'm sick of the sight of those tired
old shorts and that dreary T-shirt. Get inside — this minute!
Jan (*taking the lettuce and going indoors*) All right, but nothing fancy.

Jan exits

Eunice collects the flan from the table and follows Jan indoors

Sam She seems nice. Good company for Mum.
Charlie And, God, must she need it. Stuck down here with the old man and
Hettie.
Sam (*to Miles*) Want your drink, darling? (*She produces a can of soft drink
from her bag and a packet of cigarettes and a lighter*)

Miles, still holding the ball, comes and sits on the ground beside his mother

Miles Cards.
Sam (*taking a pack of cards from her bag*) There we are.

*Sam lights a cigarette and Miles starts to play a "game" of sorts by himself,
now and then handing a card to his mother*

Takes you back, doesn't it? Sitting out here. Long hot summer days.
Nothing to do. Happy times, weren't they ...?
Charlie (*deep in thought*) Were they? We were kids. Blissfully ignorant.

The sound of distant seagulls is heard

Sam Oh, do cheer up, for God's sake. This is Dad's party, remember.
Charlie I could have done without it.

Sam Just *try* to look happy — if only for Mum's sake.
Charlie I'm thinking of leaving her, Sam.
Sam Oh dear ... Must we?
Charlie What's the point of hanging on? We hate each other.
Sam I don't want to know, Charlie. We all have our problems.
Charlie What problems have you got? Tim's all right, isn't he?
Sam Isn't that just typical of you? (*She lowers her voice*) Of course Tim isn't bloody all right!

Miles looks up at Sam, puzzled

Daddy's OK, darling, isn't he? (*She glares at Charlie*)
Charlie Oh, well, I'm sorry — but I'm going to have to tell Mum at some point.
Sam Not today. Anyway, why bother her with it all?
Charlie (*rising; angrily*) Oh no — don't let's worry her. Of course, if this was Ben or you in trouble ——
Sam Oh, cut it out. Same old record. It gets boring, Charlie. Anyway, if anyone went short of motherly love it certainly wasn't you. You boys could do no wrong. Now give it a rest.

Richard appears at the back gate

Richard Ah — so this is where you all are.
Sam Hi, Dad. Don't blame us — we did tell you.
Richard Did you? When? Must have forgotten. I do that. Never mind — it's all good exercise for me. (*To Miles, delighted to see him*) Miles, old chap. This is a nice surprise. I thought we weren't going to see you. (*He bends and kisses Miles*)
Sam Happy birthday, Dad. No presents till later. He's got you something really special, haven't you, Miles?
Richard Well, of course he has: he loves his poor old grandpa, don't you, lad?
Charlie (*hugging Richard*) Happy birthday, Dad. Sorry about the mix-up.
Richard Not to worry. I simply wanted to save you the expense of bringing the car across.
Charlie Ben offered to pay, but guess what — he didn't show up.
Richard (*sitting on a bench at the table*) Oh dear. Told your mother?
Sam He'll come. We know Ben by now. Likes to make an entrance. He'll arrive bearing the most expensive present and a bottle of champagne.
Charlie I put the car in the garage and nearly wrenched my bloody arm off.
Richard I know — I know. I'm an artiste, boy. I'm not into all that do-it-yourself nonsense.
Charlie Mother's gone and decorated the den, I see. That's a first.
Richard Had to. We've no money to chuck around getting in professionals.

Sam (*rising*) I must have a look — I haven't seen it.

Sam goes indoors

Miles throws the ball to Richard and they throw it back and forth during the following

Richard I hope Ben does come. Ruin your mother's day if he doesn't.
Charlie (*picking up a paper to read*) Really? Personally I couldn't give a toss.
Richard He isn't staying away because of you I hope.

No answer

You're still not speaking I take it. Oh, Charlie — life's too short for all this. It breaks your mother's heart.
Charlie Don't tell me, Dad. Tell him. He started it.
Richard Oh, grow up. Be your age for heaven's sake!
Charlie Always my fault, you see. Pain-in-the-arse Charlie.
Richard Well, it's ridiculous.
Charlie (*ready for a row*) Look, Dad ——

Sam comes storming out of the house

Sam It's dreadful! Quite ghastly! Whatever possessed you, Dad?
Richard Nothing to do with me. It was your mother. "Time for a change," she said. "Blow away the cobwebs — get with it!"
Sam It's completely out of character with the rest of the house. What do you think, Charlie ...?
Charlie (*engrossed in his paper*) What ...?
Sam And where are all your books? The pictures, your scripts?
Richard She's cleaning them, I expect. How do I know? It is our house, Sam. We are allowed to decorate it as we wish.
Sam But not the den. That's our past, our family history. All our memories were in that room.
Richard We try not to live in the past; we try desperately to live now and things have to change. Anyway, your mother likes it.
Sam (*peevishly, childishly*) She must have lost her marbles, then, if that's what she regards as "getting with it!"
Richard (*annoyed, sharply*) Sam — give it a rest, please.
Sam OK. Mind your own business, Sam. You don't live here any more.
Richard Precisely!

Eunice appears from the house, all smiles

Eunice Are you ready for this, folks? Presenting Miss Isle of Wight — 1966!

Jan, looking slightly sheepish, comes out looking different in a summer dress. She is nicely but simply made up, her hair has been deftly rearranged

Jan smiles but nothing happens; the others are all preoccupied. Richard and Miles continue throwing the ball back and forth

Jan I told you, Eunice — I could step out here stark naked and they wouldn't notice.
Richard You look lovely, darling.
Jan Thank you. Now — shall we plan the day ...?
Charlie (*rising*) I'm going in for a shower — OK?
Jan (*aware of an atmosphere*) Of course, darling: clean towels in the airing cupboard ...

Charlie exits into the house

Sam Come with Mummy, Miles. We'll get the presents from the car.
Miles (*thrilled*) Yeah ...!

Sam and Miles leave by the back gate

Jan What on earth's been going on?
Richard Don't ask.
Jan I see.
Eunice (*collecting the Pimms tray*) The chilled white wine first, or more Pimms?
Jan We'll leave it to you, Eunice, you're the expert.
Eunice (*heading into the house*) Oh, the excitement of it all. I adore other people's birthdays.

Eunice exits

Jan There's an atmosphere already — I can sense it.
Richard It's nothing. (*He holds his arms outstretched*) Come here.

Jan and Richard meet C. *Richard folds his arms around Jan*

Jan (*contentedly*) Happy birthday.
Richard You've said that twice already.
Jan I can say it as often as I wish.
Richard Thank you. (*He kisses her head*) You look lovely — and you smell divine.

Jan It's all Eunice. She means well. (*Beat*) No Ben.

Richard I know. What a bore. No phone call?

Jan Zilch! How are things otherwise?

Richard Touch and go. Was all this a very good idea?

Jan Charlie's still on about Ben, I suppose.

Richard Afraid so. And Sam hates the den. Obviously you should have consulted her.

Jan (*laughing*) Whatever for? We don't interfere in her life. Oh God — how frail a thing is parenthood.

Richard I've told you, hundreds of times, you worry too much about them.

Jan I'm their mother; that's what mothers do. (*Beat*) Richard, you are happy, aren't you?

Richard Of course I am. I'd prefer there were just the two of us. Especially today.

Jan It seemed like a good idea. At the time. One last birthday party.

Richard Last ...?

Hettie Oh, Richard — I didn't mean that!

Richard (*laughing*) I know what you meant. But let's face it — there can't be that much time left.

Jan (*moving away*) Don't say that. I'm not listening — I refuse to listen.

Richard I was teasing ...

Jan All right, I promise you this: no more parties until you're eighty — how's that? We'll spend the next ten years here alone. Go for walks, drink tea, play endless rounds of cards with Hettie and Eunice ...

Richard At least Eunice goes home at nights.

Jan Yes, well, I'm going to stop complaining. (*She looks up at the house*) We really must get that guttering fixed before the winter sets in.

Richard laughs again

It's not funny, Richard.

Richard (*sincerely*) Standing there, in this light, dressed like that, you could be twenty-five again.

Jan Oh, stop it ...

Richard We could always creep away, leave them to it, go to bed, lock the door.

Jan That would sound delightful if I didn't know all you had in mind was sleeping.

Richard can't help but look slightly wounded

Oh — I've done it again! I was joking, Richard.

Richard Am I a great disappointment?

During the following, Jan tucks Richard's arms around her again

No. Never. It was a joke. I love you, Richard — even though you're ancient.

Jan kisses Richard warmly

Richard ...?
Richard Yes? What have you done now ...?
Jan The den.
Richard What about it ...?
Jan You do like it, don't you?
Richard I love it. Very clean and tidy — but we can live with that.
Jan It's just that ——

Hettie enters on to the patio and is at once embarrassed by Jan's and Richard's outward show of affection. She coughs politely

Richard Hettie, dearest. Come and join us. We were about to crack open the chilled white wine and strip off ...!
Hettie (*coldly*) Not for me — thank you ...!

The Lights fade. Music fills the auditorium

We move as smoothly and as quickly as possible into the next scene

Jan and Richard exit

Miles enters

Miles and Hettie sit at the dining-table

The Lights come back up. It is about half an hour later

Hettie and Miles are playing cards. Hettie is dealing; Miles picks up the cards as she deals

The music fades

Hettie (*dealing cards*) Now, I have seven cards, and you have seven cards — do you follow?
Miles (*picking up cards*) Yes.
Hettie Ah, naughty, naughty — wait until I've dealt.

Eunice enters with two large bowls of salad which she places on the table in front of Miles and Hettie

Eunice Time to move, Hettie, dear — soon be lunch. (*She goes back indoors*)
Hettie Ignore the woman, Miles — I do. Now, the fifteenth card, as it were, I turn over — like so — do you understand ...?
Miles (*already ahead of her*) Yes.

Jan comes out with plates etc. which she lays on the table.

Jan Lunch, Hettie — please.
Hettie Anything I can do ...?
Jan You could move, dear — over there, perhaps.

Jan goes off again

Hettie I used to play cards all the time with my dead husband.

Miles looks at her

Well, he wasn't dead then, of course. Now, do you need that card? You have to get ... Look, I'll show you my cards — I have to get four of the same suit — and three of another ... Look — show me your cards — put them down on the table ...

Miles refuses to do this and holds his cards close to his chest

Eunice comes out carrying two bottles of red wine and two of white — all already opened

Eunice The booze, Hettie.
Hettie (*coldly*) I don't drink, thank you.
Eunice (*putting the wine on the table*) Oh no — of course you don't ...

Eunice exits into the house

Hettie Now don't be silly, Miles, show me your hand.

Jan enters from the house with wine glasses etc.

This boy seems to cotton on remarkably quickly.
Jan He's autistic, Hettie, not stupid! Now, please.
Hettie (*to Miles*) If you don't show me your cards, how can I teach you the game ...?

Jan heads for the house

Jan (*calling*) Lunch everyone — please!

Jan exits

Miles, refusing to show his cards, rises and moves over to the lounger

Hettie (*rising and moving after Miles*) Now, Miles, don't be silly. We shall
have to start all over again — you've seen my cards now.

Miles moves again to avoid Hettie. This time he sits at the small table DL.
Hettie follows him there

> *Jan and Eunice enter carrying glasses, cutlery, napkins etc.They arrange
> everything on the table during the following*

Look, are we going to play this game or not, young man?

Miles reluctantly hands over his cards to Hettie

Good; now we shall have to deal all over again.

*Miles and Hettie sit at the small table. Hettie shuffles the cards and deals
again*

Eunice (*working at the big table*) Wonder of wonders — Hettie seems to
have found a friend.
Jan (*setting glasses etc.*) It won't last — she gets far too bossy if she loses.
Hettie I can hear you. (*To Miles*) They won't play with me because I never
lose.

> *Charlie comes out of the house carrying several birthday presents wrapped
> in fancy paper: he looks freshly bathed and is wearing a pair of baggy
> shorts and a T-shirt.*

Charlie Right, our presents — me, Kay and the kids. Over here — right? (*He
lays them down on a chair on the terrace*).
Jan That's fine — he can open them when Ben gets here — *if* he ever does.
What pretty shorts, dear. Your dad's ...?
Charlie Only because it's so bloody hot. I'm not a shorts person as you know.
Jan (*teasingly*) They're very becoming, don't you think, Eunice?
Eunice I daren't look; men's naked legs drive me wild with desire ...!
Charlie Can I stick to beer?
Eunice Beer! When we have the most exclusive wines on the table? You've
raised a Philistine, Jan.

Charlie gives Eunice a dirty look and goes off indoors

Eunice Oh dear — he's not amused. Have I upset him?
Jan Leave him. My son was born without a sense of humour, I'm afraid.
Eunice He has got a certain something, though. Is he *happily* married?
Jan Very — so hands off. Sam's the only one with problems in that department.
Eunice (*polishing wine glasses*) And Ben has no problems.
Jan Not as far as I know.
Eunice Stinking rich, not married, and as free as air. Sounds too good to be true. He's probably gay — the best-looking men usually are.
Jan (*laughing, busy at the table*) Oh, stop it!
Eunice It's true. Look at Lex up at the tennis club. I spent ages trying to get him into bed but all to no avail. Apparently he lives with Mario, the barman. We've forgotten the bread.

Jan stops working, her mind suddenly on something else

Jan (*as if thunderstruck*) You know, it's never even crossed my mind. (*She sits*) Isn't that awful?
Eunice What's awful? What have I said now?
Jan I mean — Ben's just Ben, isn't he?
Eunice You've lost me, dear.
Jan I'm his mother for heaven's sake — mothers are supposed to know these things. Could he be gay, do you think?
Eunice Of course not. Oh, here we go — me and my big mouth. (*She pours Jan some red wine*) Here, a glass of red wine: it's supposed to stimulate the heart.
Jan I've never ever considered the possibility. I feel terrible, Eunice.
Eunice Well, don't. It was just a flippant remark; I wasn't being serious. Anyway, obviously you'd have noticed if he was ... well ...
Jan But how? I never see him. I mean, he phones — once a week he phones — he pays for Richard and me to go abroad every year, he's wildly generous. Is that a sign of something?
Eunice Don't be ridiculous. (*Worriedly*) Does he keep sending you flowers and things ...?
Jan Never. He can't even remember my birthday, let alone Richard's.
Eunice There you are then.
Jan What?
Eunice Definitely not gay.
Jan Are you sure?
Eunice He's had girlfriends, hasn't he?
Jan Of course.
Eunice You see!

Jan When he was nine or ten. I'm not sure about since ... Oh, my God! (*She gulps down the wine*)
Eunice Now, just stop all this — you're being silly. They should put me away; I always, always say the wrong thing. More wine?
Jan Good God, no! I shall be drunk.

At the small table, Miles lays down his cards

Hettie You haven't won already! That's nonsense. (*She inspects Miles's cards*) Beginner's luck. It can't happen again. (*She collects the cards*) I'll put a stop to this. (*Calling over to Jan*) This boy may be backward but he knows how to cheat!
Jan (*firmly, annoyed*) He is *not* backward, Hettie!

Hettie gives Jan a cold stare and starts to reshuffle the cards

Eunice (*lowering her voice*) Calm down, calm down.
Jan I wonder if Sam knows. Or Charlie. I'm going to have to ask him, now, before we have lunch.
Eunice Is that wise?
Jan I have to know, Eunice. Maybe that's why they fell out — maybe ——
Eunice Jan, I'm warning you: I shall slap your wrists if this continues.

Sam appears at the back gate, hot and breathless from her walk

Sam Sorry — I got lost. I thought I knew my way around here.
Jan (*deep in thought*) Sorry, dear ...?
Eunice I'll get the bread and then I think we're ready to eat. Excuse me.

Eunice gives Jan a worried look and exits into the house

Sam What happened to Hardy's Wood? Half of it's disappeared. Are you all right?
Jan I'm fine. I think. Hardy's Wood? They built a supermarket on it. If it isn't owned by the National Trust, they build on it. Nice walk, dear? (*She busies herself at the table again, folding napkins*)
Sam Don't the locals protest about all these changes?
Jan Sometimes — but apparently it's all down to money.
Sam Well, if I lived here ——
Jan Yes, well you don't. And things will change — with or without your permission.
Sam (*moving over to the card game*) What's going on here, then?
Hettie Your son's fast becoming a sharp card-player.

Sam I'm not surprised. He has a fantastic memory. (*She sees Hettie's cards*)
Hettie's got four Queens.
Hettie Samantha — really!

Sam goes back to her mother, puts her arms around her and kisses her head

Sam I'm sorry, Mum. I'm a grumpy old sod at times, aren't I?
Jan Darling, of course you're not.
Sam Eunice is nice, isn't she? (*She sits at the table*)
Jan Very. My saviour during the winter. I could leave Richard in front of the
telly, Hettie in her room and ... you know ... and pop round to Eunice for
a glass of wine and a laugh. She's made me realize just how lonely I've
become.
Sam Lonely?
Jan Well, not lonely exactly. Isolated perhaps. Stagnant. I mean, where do
we ever go? Who do we see?
Sam Has Dad become difficult?
Jan Of course he hasn't.
Sam Mum — this is me you're talking to.
Jan I just worry. Especially after ... Well, you know. (*To change the subject*)
Now what about you?
Sam There's nothing to tell. You know, on my walk just now, I realized just
how much I miss the island.
Jan Oh, rubbish. Two days and you'd be screaming to get back.
Sam To what, though?
Jan (*taking Sam's hand*) Oh now. We all become discontent at times. It
happens, love. And we're not immune to it across here.
Sam You're not unhappy, are you?
Jan Of course not ...
Sam You've everything you want. This wonderful house ——
Jan Which is falling down about our ears.
Sam There's Dad, who loves you to death.
Jan Who's becoming so vague I often wonder if he even knows I'm here.
Sam He's getting old, that's all. And you're not.
Jan It has nothing to do with the difference in our ages. It's just so sad that
his heart attack put an end to his career.
Sam He could always go back.
Jan I've heard him on the phone. I've seen the letters of rejection. They've
forgotten him, Sam. So every day seems to get longer ... He sits about;
watches endless re-runs on telly; he's no good in the garden; he can't *make*
things. He was a cinematographer, for heaven's sake. He misses the buzz,
the gossip, the film stars.
Sam All his signed photographs in the den, his original scripts — what's
happened to them? They must be worth a fortune.

Jan rises, on edge; during the following she tries not to cry

Jan Look, it's time we had lunch. Ben is obviously not going to show up. Oh, why must he be like this? He's so childish. (*She puts a napkin to her face to hide her tears*)
Sam (*moving to Jan, concerned*) Mum? Mum — what is it?
Jan (*drying her eyes*) Look, please — don't let Hettie see. I'm fine — honestly.
Hettie (*aware of something, calling over to Sam*) Is she all right ...?
Sam Something in her eye, that's all.
Hettie I think I've got the better of this lad. (*She lays down her cards*) I've won! Just one more game — then it's lunch.

Miles shuffles the cards this time

Jan (*to Sam, quietly*) You'd think he'd have made the bloody effort, wouldn't you?
Sam He'll turn up; you know how he loves to be the centre of attention.
Jan But today of all days. Maybe I just don't really know anything about him.
Sam What's that supposed to mean?
Jan Have I been a terrible mother?
Sam (*laughing*) What's brought all this on? You've been a wonderful mother.
Jan Oh yes. Wonderful. Two of my children believe I loved the third better than either of them.
Sam You loved the boys more than me — you can't deny that.

A telephone rings in the house

Jan You see. That is simply not true. I loved you all equally. Is that the phone?
Sam Someone will get it. Relax. Why are you so jumpy?

The phone stops ringing during the following

Jan I'm in such a mess.
Sam You're being quite ridiculous, Mother. Now, come on, out with it; what's really troubling you?
Jan It's this party, I suppose. You know I've always hated arranging parties. (*Beat*) Sam ...?
Sam What?
Jan About Ben.
Sam What about Ben?
Jan Do you ever see him?

Sam See him? Not very often — why?
Jan It's just that ...

Richard comes out of the house talking into the mobile house phone

Richard I can imagine — yes. ... Well, she's here now; have a word with her.

Richard hands the phone to Jan

Jan (*mouthing the words*) Who is it? (*Into the phone*) Hallo? (*Delightedly*)
Ben! (*Then angry*) Don't tell me — you can't manage it! ... You can! Then
where the hell are you? We're about to start lunch. ... You're on the ferry
now: that's wonderful! ... All right — but do try to hurry. ... You've what?
... Well, that's fine. Who is it — a girlfriend? ... Oh, I see — right. Well,
we shall look forward to meeting him.

Eunice enters from the house carrying some bread and a knife

(*Into the phone*) Yes, of course, dear. See you soon. Bye.

Charlie comes out on to the terrace, a can of beer in his hand

Richard Well ...?

Jan hands the phone back to Richard

Jan He's on his way ... and he's bringing a guest. (*With a look at Eunice*) A
man.
Eunice (*dropping the bread knife*) A man ...?
Richard A man. Well, that's good. The more the merrier. How say you?
Charlie What man's this then?
Jan (*trying to be light*) Who knows — a "friend", I imagine.
Eunice How nice.
Charlie (*moving to the lounger*) He's got a bloody cheek, hasn't he!
Richard Now Charles.
Charlie (*sitting*) Husbands, wives, grandchildren not invited to the celebra-
tions — total stranger welcome.
Jan Charlie, stop it! You're embarrassing Eunice.
Eunice (*confusedly*) Is he? Look — I'd hate to be in the way. I can always
go back to my virgin couch and watch Wimbledon.
Jan (*rising, trying to lighten the mood*) Nonsense. You're part of the family.
Right, lunch in ten minutes. We've waited long enough. Richard, off with
that disgusting shirt and on with a clean one.

Richard Oh Lord, must I?
Jan It's your birthday and if I can make the effort so can you.
Richard I'm going, I'm going.

Richard exits into the house

Eunice (*following Richard*) I'll pop the champagne into the fridge and take out the strawberries.

Eunice exits

Sam (*moving over to Miles*) Come along, darling — time to wash our hands.

Miles pulls a face

You can play cards with Hettie later. Hands!

Sam and Miles go off into the house

Hettie (*rising*) I'll get my mineral water and bring it to the table.
Jan Unless you'd rather have wine; it is a special occasion.
Hettie (*heading into the house*) I'll stick to water, thank you.

Hettie exits

Jan She'll pop up to her room now for a quick "nip" to see her through lunch.
Charlie Quite sad, I suppose — the games people play.
Jan We all play games, Charlie. And as long as we know the rules, no-one gets hurt. (*She moves over to Charlie*) How's Kay?
Charlie Kay? What about her?
Jan What do you mean "What about her?" I'm asking.
Charlie Kay's Kay — she's fine. Still attending keep fat classes.
Jan (*slapping Charlie*) There's no need to be cruel. Are you sure she's fine?
Charlie Do stop fishing, Mother. As you've already said, let's have a nice day.
Jan I suppose you were hoping he wouldn't come.
Charlie Let him come. I shan't speak to him.
Jan (*raising her eyes to heaven and moving away*) Honestly — what are you like? (*Beat*) Charles ...?
Charlie Oh, here we go.
Jan What ...?
Charlie You only ever call me Charles when you're angry or when you're after something: which is it?

Jan The trouble between you and Ben: what was it about?

Charlie None of your business.

Jan It wasn't to do with ... (*She makes a gesture*)

Charlie (*repeating the gesture, amused*) With what?

Jan Well, now, how can I put this delicately? It wasn't, for instance, anything to do with his private life, was it?

Charlie Ben's private life has nothing to do with me. Just as long as he stays out of mine.

Jan Meaning what?

Charlie Meaning — people in glass houses and all that.

Jan Is that supposed to have some significance?

Charlie Look, Mum, I don't need all this. Now can we leave it?

Jan Why can I never get a simple answer to a simple question out of you two? I'm your mother, for heaven's sake!

Charlie Yes, and there are some things you're better off not knowing ... Now can we drop the subject, please.

Jan He isn't involved in anything shady, is he? It would kill your father.

Charlie You know what he does.

Jan Yes, but outside of his business, his colleagues, his relationships, has he any — chums?

Charlie (*finding this very funny*) Chums? What the hell's the matter with you today?

Jan It isn't funny — I need to know these things. I mean ... Well, why has he never married?

Charlie Why don't you ask him? You must just thank God he never did. He could have been leading some poor woman a dog's life all these years.

Jan Now that's unkind. He'd make a wonderful husband. He's kind, considerate, wildly generous. I'd be delighted to be married to Ben.

Charlie Then marry him. I've always thought your love for him was a bit unnatural anyway.

Jan Charles! Don't be disgusting!

Charlie Mother, I'm warning you, all this is leading nowhere. I have no interest whatsoever in what my brother does, where he goes, or to whom he grants his sexual favours. (*Rising*) Now where's this lunch? I'm starving.

Jan This is a conspiracy, isn't it? You and Sam have conspired to keep me in the dark. It's a deliberate attempt to pull the wool over my eyes.

Charlie (*helping himself to food*) You're pissed. I can tell. Too much sun and too many poncy Pimms.

Jan I should have been told; you have no right to deceive me in this way.

Charlie It's none of my business to tell you anything. If Ben wishes to keep up a front for you and Dad then so be it.

Jan (*in panic now*) I must find Richard; we can't have all this blurted out on his birthday. (*She rushes towards the house*) We have a crisis!

Eunice enters from the house bearing a bowl of fruit

Eunice Fruit, anybody ...?

Jan rushes off

Eunice watches Jan go

Now what's the matter with her?
Charlie It seems she's been doing her sums at last, putting two and two together. Ben.
Eunice Oh, Lord, this is all my fault.

Hettie comes out carrying a bottle of mineral water

Charlie takes his plate of food and a beer back to the lounger and sits

Hettie Is Janet unwell?
Eunice A spot of hay fever, I think. She'll be fine. (*She sits at the table*)

Hettie sits at the table

Richard comes storming out of the house, now wearing a clean shirt and trousers

Richard (*furiously*) I will not have your mother upset on my birthday. What have you said to her, Charlie?
Charlie (*amused*) I haven't said anything.
Richard She simply said "Prepare yourself for a shock", burst into tears and fled into the bathroom. Now what's going on here?
Charlie Storms and teacups, Father — it'll all blow over. She's got it into her head that Ben might be gay.
Richard Oh, I see. (*He does a double-take*) What?
Charlie Gay, Father. A bum-bandit.
Hettie This is revolting!
Richard Shut up, Hettie! Ben? A homosexual?
Hettie Richard! We have a child in the house!
Eunice (*hiding her face in shame*) Oh, Eunice, Eunice!
Richard Is this all your doing, Eunice? Only since you came to the island has my wife been coming out with these outrageous statements.
Eunice I'm sorry, Richard — all I said was ——
Richard Now, I demand to know — is my son gay or not?

Sam and Miles enter. They each carry a wrapped present for Richard

Sam (*quite calmly*) I don't know, Dad, you'll have to ask him. Charlie — are you gay or not?

Charlie, busy eating, raises two fingers

Sam (*to Miles*) Sit at the table, darling.
Eunice (*rising*) Had I better see to her?
Richard Please ... Be a sweetheart, Eunice.

Eunice goes indoors

Richard (*almost to himself*) Well, I'll be buggered!
Hettie Richard! Not in front of the boy!
Sam (*putting food on a plate for Miles*) Anyway, would it matter?
Richard Well, of course it would matter. All these years we've thought of him as one thing and he turns out to be the other.
Sam We don't know that. He's never said anything to me.
Richard Have you ever asked him?
Sam Of course not — why should I?
Charlie (*enjoying all the fuss*) Perhaps this chap he's bringing will turn out to be his chum. Perhaps it's a day for true love confessions.
Sam (*laughing*) A "coming-out" ball.
Hettie I don't think this is anything to laugh about, Samantha.
Sam No, Hettie? We could all do with a bloody good laugh at something. Now can we eat, please?

Sam gives Miles his food and helps herself

Eunice comes out with Jan who is wiping her eyes

Eunice She's fine now, aren't you, dear?
Jan Eunice says you all know.
Richard We only know what we *think* we know; in fact we know nothing at all.
Jan I don't want a word of all this when he arrives. Not a word. We shall all pretend we haven't a clue. Promise?
Sam (*tucking into her food*) Come and eat, Mother; stop fussing.
Jan If, eventually, in time, he wishes it to be known, we shall act surprised — right?

Richard, Sam and Charlie all act mock-surprised

Jan Please, this is serious. I mean — what if this "friend" he's bringing is ... ?

Charlie That's what I said. Now could we please talk about something else? It's putting me off my food.

Jan Charlie, do sit at the table.

Charlie I'm OK — cooler over here.

Eunice and Jan join the others at the table

Richard (*taking his place at the head of the table*) Now tuck in everybody. Feel free to gorge yourselves.

Eunice (*pouring wine for everyone*) Red or white? We have an abundance of both.

Hettie (*helping herself to food*) Not for me, thank you.

They all start to eat

Miles whispers something to his mother

Sam Not now, darling. After lunch, eh? Oh, all right — if you must.

Miles rises, picks up a present and gives it to Richard

Miles Happy birthday, Grandpa.

Delighted, everyone applauds Miles

Richard (*kissing the boy on the head, touched*) For me? Why, thank you, my boy. Open it now, shall I? (*He removes the wrapping from a huge heavy book entitled "Chronicle of the Cinema — 100 Years of the Movies"*) Oh, I say. What a wonderful present. Look everyone. (*He holds the book up*)

Sam He was thrilled, Dad. It mentions you at least a dozen times.

Richard I shall read it from cover to cover, Miles. In fact, it's the very best present I've ever had. I shall add it to my collection. (*To Jan*) Isn't this a wonderful book, darling?

Jan looks uneasy and does not answer

Now, I shall propose the first toast of the day. (*He rises, glass in hand*) To my guests, for taking the trouble to come to my party; to Eunice who, when she isn't filling my wife's head with nonsense, has become a valued neighbour and a true friend; and, finally, to my beautiful wife Jan — come on, take a bow ——

Richard gets Jan up on her feet

— without whom I could never have reached this great age. Cheers, everyone.

They all raise their glasses except for Jan

All Cheers. Happy birthday. (*Etc., etc.*)

Richard sits again and starts helping himself to food while the others drink and eat. Jan remains standing

Jan (*unable to contain herself any longer*) I sold them, Richard.
Richard Sorry, dear ...?
Jan You may as well all know. Your father's collection of signed photo-graphs in the den, his film books, his original manuscripts: I told you I'd stored them away in the attic, Richard. Well, I didn't. I was offered five thousand pounds for them and I accepted.

There is a stunned silence

Sam (*is this a joke?*) You're not serious ...?
Jan Don't ask what possessed me. I did it. So there. I'm sorry, Richard.

No-one knows what to say

Jan Well, say something — anyone.
Sam The signed Astaire? The Brando? The Monroe and the Sinatra, plus God knows how many hundreds more, Mum? You *sold* them!
Jan I did. I sold them.
Sam (*rising from the table*) Tell me I'm not hearing this.
Richard Sam, shut up.
Sam At least a dozen of those photographs were autographed to me, Dad. We were with you on location, remember. The Elizabeth Taylor/Richard Burton were mine.
Richard I said shut up, Sam!
Sam Can you hear what she's saying ...?
Richard I shall not tell you again, Sam — now keep quiet. (*Beat*) All those photographs, the books, the scripts, in fact every piece of that collection was officially mine. If your mother, for whatever reason, has decided to be rid of them, then that's her choice.
Sam (*lighting a cigarette*) But for *five* thousand pounds! The movie scripts alone — signed by the entire cast and crew, remember — would have fetched four, five, ten times that!

Richard (*banging his fist on the table*) Sam! I'm warning you!

There is an awful silence

Jan (*quietly*) The roof's leaking, the boiler's on its last legs, the whole house needs re-wiring: it all has to be paid for.
Sam I can't believe this. You're not telling us you're short of money?
Charlie And Dad's pension: what about that?
Jan What pension? Your dad was in show business.

Jan takes Richard's hand

Hettie I think I'll go to my room ...
Jan Please, Hettie — this concerns us all.
Eunice Would you like me to disappear, Jan?
Jan Please stay; I need your support, Eunice.
Sam (*to Eunice*) You knew about this?
Eunice Well ... yes.
Jan I had to confide in someone. Who else had I? I'm sorry, Richard, I really didn't know what else to do. Please forgive me.
Hettie I could have contributed; I did offer.
Jan Oh, Hettie, contributed with what? Samuel hardly left you well off, did he?
Charlie We all assumed you were more than comfortably off.
Jan Yes, Charlie. Well, it's very easy to go through life assuming.
Charlie But your foreign holidays, your trips abroad ...
Jan Ben paid for those. Ben would have paid for everything. I simply thought it wrong to ask for more.
Charlie He never told us. Did you know about this, Sam?

Sam doesn't answer

We could have helped; there really was no need to sell Dad's collection.
Richard Enough now, please. I've heard enough. If you must know, I'm the reason we're in this financial mess.
Jan No, Richard ... please don't.
Richard Jan, it's me who must take the blame. It was my foolishness. (*To the others*) Whatever money we had — in fact most of the money I'd ever earned — I squandered on some bloody stupid project I was foolish enough to have faith in. A film. A film I was going to direct. I thought "At last, this is my opportunity to do what I've always dreamed of." The film was never even made. It was a terrible idea and there was no-one else to blame but me.
Sam You lost everything?

Richard Nearly everything. I broke the first rule of show business: never invest your own money. I'm sorry, Eunice — you must be very embarrassed by all this.
Eunice I'm not at all embarrassed.

Jan turns and heads indoors

Richard Jan — please.
Jan I'm all right, Richard. At least I'm relieved to have told you.

Jan exits

Eunice (*trying to make herself useful, rising*) Miles — would you like your pudding? We've got strawberry flan, trifle, ice-cream ...
Sam Ice-cream, Eunice. He likes ice-cream.
Eunice Leave it to Aunty Eunice — she'll get it.

Eunice heads for the house, placing a friendly hand on Richard's shoulder as she passes him

Eunice exits

Silence

Richard Well, I hope you're both pleased with yourselves.
Sam Why on earth did you never tell us any of this?
Richard Oddly enough, Sam, because we care too much about you. Anyway, what business is it of yours? We knew how you'd react.
Sam And what's that supposed to mean?
Richard We knew you'd over-react. You always do.
Charlie Me? I haven't said a word.
Richard Your sister has behaved disgracefully.
Sam Oh, thanks.
Hettie (*rising*) I think I'll just ——
Richard (*losing his temper*) Oh, for Christ's sake, woman, if you're that desperate for a drink, have one! Stop all this pretending!

Silence. Hettie is deeply hurt. So is Richard

Hettie Shall we have another game, Miles? Would you like that?

Miles, who has been looking rather bewildered by all that has been said, goes over to the card table and sits

At least the boy knows how to behave in a civilized fashion. He's a credit to you, Samantha.

Hettie joins Miles at the table. Miles deals cards during the following

Sam It's a day for revelations obviously. Your birthday's turned into a battle-field, Dad.
Richard Nonsense. I'm happy. They were only bloody photographs for heaven's sake. Left-overs from a forgotten age. Who cares about old movies any more?
Sam You'd be surprised. They were your past, your life. You don't think she's sold your Oscar as well ...?
Richard Of course she hasn't. That Oscar is propping open the lavatory door at this very moment.
Charlie (*rising and moving to the table to refill his plate*) Fancy old Benny-boy paying for all those holidays. I'm sort of impressed. Much against my better nature, of course.
Sam Oh, give us a break. Anyway, he can afford it. He can pay for me and Miles to go to Barbados if he likes.

Ben appears at the back gate, a bottle of champagne in one hand, a bouquet of flowers in the other

Ben Sister dear — it would be a pleasure. In fact, why don't we all go to Barbados?
Charlie Oh, my God! Kill the fatted calf — he's arrived. Only three hours late, of course!

Richard rises, thrilled to see Ben

Richard Ben! My dear boy — welcome.
Ben (*embracing his father warmly*) Happy birthday, Pa. How old are you? Ninety is it?
Richard I prefer not to count. (*He takes the champagne*) For me?
Ben And the flowers — didn't know what else to get you. (*He kisses Richard*) Sorry I missed the ferry, Sam. (*He kisses Sam*) Charlie! Old thing!

Charlie turns away and ignores Ben

And who do I see? My little nephew. I didn't expect you to be here. What's all this? Teaching the boy to gamble already, Hettie?
Hettie We've been talking about you, young man.
Sam Hettie ... !

Ben I'm sure you have. Everyone talks about me, Hettie. My good looks, my charm, my money!
Charlie Your modesty.
Ben Oh, that above all else, brother dear. And how's the little wife these days?

Charlie gives Ben a look of contempt

Brice appears at the back gate looking slightly ill-at-ease. Craggy, tanned, untidy of dress and unshaven, he has a look of the "flower-power" era about him, with torn jeans and beads around his neck: all of this, rather than dating him, gives him a somewhat individual, distinctive quality — one might feel immediately comfortable in his company

Richard Ah, your friend. Do come in, sir. You are most welcome.
Charlie My God — who the hell's this?
Richard (*taking Brice's hand*) Have we met? The face seems vaguely familiar.
Brice You must be Richard.
Richard Indeed I am. And you are?

Brice looks to Ben as if in need of help or support

Ben Ah, yes: our mystery guest — unknown to all but one of us — well, two of us to be absolutely accurate. The birthday surprise, Dad. A pleasant one, I trust. He's a nice chap, fond of sailing — loves the sea. Thought I'd bring him across with me. We could hire a boat, have some fun, all of us maybe — one big happy family!

Jan enters from the house

Jan Apologies all round — I seem to mistime everything. (*Thrilled to see Ben*) Ben! You're here! And who's this ...?
Brice (*turning to look at her*) Hallo, Jan.
Jan (*pale, hand to mouth*) God in heaven ...!
Brice It's been a long time.
Jan Brice? What the hell ...? I think I'm going to be sick.
Richard May one ask what is going on?
Ben (*putting a hand round Brice's shoulder and grinning*) Sam, Charlie, I'd like you to meet our father ... Our *real* father, that is.

Eunice appears on the patio with a tray of puddings

Eunice Ice cream, anyone, trifle ...?

The Lights fade quickly to Black-out

ACT II

The same. Later that afternoon

When the scene begins, the garden is now partly in shadow. The table has been cleared except for a bowl of fruit, but all the presents still lie unopened on the terrace

We can still hear the sea and seagulls in the distance

After a moment, Brice comes out on to the terrace rolling a cigarette, something he's done all his life. He turns and looks back at the den, then comes DS and looks at the "view"

After a moment, Hettie appears on the terrace, sees Brice, and disappears back into the house again

Brice, quietly amused, lights his cigarette

Eunice enters from the house

Eunice Ahh ...
Brice Can I help ...?
Eunice We were wondering if Janet was about.
Brice About ...?
Eunice Out here. But obviously not.
Brice I believe she's taken the boy for a walk. Miles?
Eunice Yes. Yes, Miles. I was about to make a cup of tea — that's all. (*She turns to go*)
Brice Oh yes, please. I'd love some tea.
Eunice Oh. Right. Well ...

Eunice disappears indoors

Again, Brice smiles to himself

After a while, Richard comes out and stops, feeling rather awkward

Richard Ahh ...

Brice Ahh ...
Richard No Jan.
Brice 'Fraid not. (*Beat*) Wonderful view.
Richard (*moving* DS) Indeed. We do our best to please. (*Beat*) I do hope you
don't think we're trying to ignore you.
Brice Aren't you? Can't be easy.
Richard Precisely. Not for any of us. Except for Ben, of course.
Brice (*with a laugh*) Ah, yes. Ben. I think Ben is far too confident to be fazed
by anything.
Richard Quite.
Brice (*taking a deep breath of air*) Just taste that fresh air. "The air on the
Downs is worth sixpence a pint!" Didn't someone once say that?
Richard Tennyson. Probably standing where you are now. (*Beat*) I have no
wish to be rude, old boy, but may one ask: why exactly did you come back?
Not to rock any boats, I hope.
Brice Not at all. Perhaps to make sure the boat is safely secured in harbour.

The two men look at each other

Brice Are those The Needles out there?
Richard No. Stag and Mermaid rocks. The Needles are elsewhere. A
common error.
Brice I'm afraid I've put rather a damper on things. Spoiled your party.
Richard Not at all. (*Beat*) How did Ben come across you?
Brice I'm sure he'll tell you. I hope he will. None of this was my idea.
Richard Oh, I can believe that. He's always had a rather mischievous streak.
Well, I'm sure you know.
Brice Actually, no. I haven't seen him for over thirty years.
Richard No. No, of course not.

Ben comes out carrying a glass of wine

Ben Ahh, here you both are. I've been showing Dad the rest of the house,
Dad. Everything all right?
Richard I was just telling your father ....
Brice (*sitting on the lounger*) Brice, please — it's easier.
Richard I was just telling Brice what a devil you can be. Always up to
mischief.
Ben Not any more, Dad. As a kid maybe. Straight as a die now.

Ben hands the glass of wine to Brice

As you appear not to want to mingle with the others, I've brought you this.

Brice Thank you.

Richard (*ill at ease*) Yes, well, I'll just pop back. Mustn't neglect my other guests. (*He attempts a little laugh*)

Richard exits indoors

Ben (*laughing*) Oh dear.

Brice I don't think this was wise.

Ben Bollocks — it's fun. Spoken to Mum yet?

Brice No. She keeps trying to avoid me. You could say she looks rather put out — not to mention embarrassed.

Ben Give her time. You know Mum.

Brice I'm not sure I do any more. It's been a long time.

Ben She hasn't changed all that much.

Brice Richard's been questioning me.

Ben Well, he would. Said anything?

Brice Not a word. I'm leaving that to you. Couldn't we just disappear for a while? Allow the dust to settle.

Ben Fancy a walk? I'll show you round the bay.

Brice OK. Why not? (*He gulps down his wine*)

Ben Good God! You're not a lush are you?

Brice (*rising*) Can't stand wine. Hate the taste. (*He puts the empty glass on the table*) Come on.

Brice and Ben head for the back gate

Ben I'll show you the rock pools — and where we used to build a camp fire. Catch a few crabs perhaps ...

They disappear from view; we hear them laughing

Richard, who has obviously been listening, enters from the house, watches Ben and Brice go and then closes the gate

Eunice enters from the house with a mug of tea

Eunice Oh — he's gone.

Richard Sorry, dear ...?

Eunice The new chap. I've brought him some tea. Only out of politeness I assure you.

Richard I'll have it. (*He takes the tea and sits*) Poor Eunice; you must be very confused.

Eunice I am. Very, very confused.

Richard (*laughing*) So am I. Where are the others?

Eunice Watching Wimbledon, though none of them seems to be enjoying it much. I think his arrival has rather upset things. Why on earth did Ben bring him here?

Richard Don't ask.

Eunice And how long has he been seeing him behind Jan's back?

Richard None of us know. No-one's hardly spoken a word.

Eunice (*sitting*) I mean — talk about a shock. I've always naturally assumed ——

Richard That they were my children?

Eunice I thought I'd got to know Jan so well. I thought we'd shared all our little secrets. But never a word about all this.

Richard No, well, why should she? To all intents and purposes I have been their father for nearly thirty years. I think Jan feels I've earned the title.

Eunice And so you have. So, let me get this straight: he just walked out and left her? With three young children?

Richard They weren't all that old themselves. Married at seventeen with Ben on the way. It was the permissive sixties; a time for losing one's inhibitions, throwing caution to the wind and all that nonsense.

Eunice How well I remember. But what a bastard!

Richard Oh, now, Eunice.

Eunice I'm sorry, Richard — but just to walk out on her like that. Was there a reason?

Richard All Jan ever told me was that he didn't feel cut out for fatherhood, so he said goodbye and set off on the hippie trail, sandals on his feet and his guitar slung over his shoulder. She did sort of hint at another woman.

Eunice Obviously. There usually is. Poor Jan.

Richard I've seen photographs of course, faded snap-shots, but other than that she's always refused to talk about him.

Eunice Did he never keep in touch? A letter — a postcard?

Richard I've no idea. I never saw any letters. Anyway, he was always abroad somewhere. He certainly looks well travelled.

Eunice Well-worn I would have said. He looks the come-to-bed type to me.

Richard I thought that was the sort you liked.

Eunice Richard ...!

Richard I'm sorry — I'm sorry.

Eunice I mean, I'd never say no — but I have to know where they've been, dear.

Richard I'm worried about Jan; has she said anything?

Eunice Not to me. She's been floating around as if everything was perfectly normal. (*She puts a hand on Richard's arm*) She loves you, Richard. She loves you with a passion. His sudden re-appearance can make no possible difference to that. (*She rises*) Oh, dear — and I wanted to like Ben so much. Why has he done this — today of all days?

Hettie comes out of the house

Hettie I'm sorry, but if I watch those balls flying back and forth any more I shall go mad.

Richard Come and join us, dear.

Hettie I do not understand you, Richard. How you can just sit about doing nothing? Why you haven't asked that dreadful person to leave this house at once. Talk about the spectre at the feast. That man was her husband.

Richard "Was", Hettie, dear — "was".

Hettie And the father of those totally inconsiderate children. You should throw him out, send for the police: they'll do it. (*She sits*)

Richard But why? What has he ever done to me? In fact, if you want the truth, I shall always be eternally grateful to the chap.

Hettie (*to heaven*) He's going mad — I know he's going mad.

Richard If he hadn't deserted Jan I may never have met her, or fallen in love with her, or married her. Now, shut up and stop fussing.

Eunice (*rising*) Tea, Hettie — I've made some.

Hettie The very last thing in the world I require is tea, thank you. I suppose this will be all over the village by nightfall.

Eunice Oh, long before that; as soon as I get home that telephone will be red hot!

Hettie Considering we have a family crisis on our hands, it seems to me a more sensitive person would have gone home anyway. Still, who am I to pass comment? Janet has already hinted that I'm nothing more than a sponger.

Richard She said nothing of the sort; you deliberately misunderstood.

Eunice (*tactfully*) Look, I'll pop home anyway. I have to feed the cats.

Richard You will come back; we need you.

Eunice You try and keep me away; we have all that champagne to get through, and your presents to open.

Eunice exits through the back gate

Richard (*gently*) Oh, come on, old girl, cheer up, eh? Things are never half as bad as they seem.

Hettie How you can put up with all this humiliation is beyond me. And how that stupid, selfish boy could even consider hurting you in this way ...

Richard Oh, I don't know; quite in character when one thinks about it. He probably thought it would be amusing, add a certain frisson to the day.

Charlie appears on the terrace, another can of beer in his hand

Charlie Six-love, six-one, six-love — it's all over. Isn't that just typical of the British players? Looking every year more mortified as they let us down yet again. (*He drinks*) Things just as miserable out here?

Richard We're fine. I was just telling Hettie — Ben probably finds all this amusing.

Charlie You bet he does. Always did have a warped sense of humour.

Richard Just leave it, Charlie, eh?

Charlie You're as bad as Mum. Let's all pretend nothing's happened; pretend everything's perfectly normal. He wanted to stir up trouble, Dad, in the same way he's always done. It gives him a sense of power to think he can alter the smooth running of things; it makes up for his deficiencies in other departments.

Richard (*losing patience*) Charlie ...!

Charlie And as for that two-bit third-rate ponce he's brought with him, a prick who just walked out and deserted us all ... Well, they deserve each other. Perhaps he's AC/DC too — perhaps that's why he left Mum ...

Richard Charlie — I'm warning you ...!

Charlie Have we ever had so much as a Christmas card from him? A birthday present? Nothing! Fuck all ...!

Jan appears at the back gate with Miles

Jan (*furiously*) Charles! I will not tolerate that kind of language in my house — or in front of this boy! (*Beat. She forces a smile*) All's well, is it? Everybody happy?

Charlie Oh yes, Mother. Delirious. Can't wait to get away from here if you must know.

Jan Then go. No-one's stopping you. In fact I'm beginning to wish I'd never asked you all to come.

Sam enters from the house

Sam Charming! (*Then to Miles, smiling*) Hallo, darling — nice walk?

Jan Lovely, wasn't it, Miles? We kept away from the madding crowds. And we saw Uncle Ben down there, didn't we?

Sam Fancy some telly, darling? Tennis — you like tennis. Come on.

Sam and Miles exit to the house

Jan (*kissing Richard's head*) Did someone make tea?

Richard Eunice. She's gone home to feed the cats.

Jan I'm not surprised. All right, Hettie?

Hettie (*rising*) Hettie's fine, thank you, Janet.

Hettie exits indoors

Jan Oh, dear. Things a bit tense, are they? (*She sits*) Well, at least it's nice and cool out here.

Richard (*taking up his crossword again*) Yes, very pleasant. Rain by
nightfall I shouldn't wonder. You OK, dear?
Jan (*trying hard not to explode*) Why shouldn't I be?
Richard I see. (*He goes back to his puzzle*) "Individual effort by Scotsman
— a wise fellow....!"

Ben appears at the back gate

Ben Ah, you're all back. I was beginning to think it was something I'd said.
Jan (*about Brice*) All alone?
Ben I've left him down there. He loves the sea, doesn't he? Seems quite
mesmerized by it.

No-one speaks

Scrabble, anyone? I Spy ...?
Charlie You've got some bloody nerve!
Ben I have indeed. It's why I'm so successful and you're not, Charlie. Nerve
and the willingness to take a risk.
Charlie Meaning what?
Jan Oh, for heaven's sake, you two. Be your age. Whatever your quarrel is
about, now is not the time.
Ben I have no quarrel with him.
Jan You just haven't spoken for six months.
Ben Correction, Mother — Charlie hasn't spoken to me for six months.
Charlie And that surprises you, does it? After what I found out.
Jan Richard, please try to be masterful and put a stop to this.
Richard I am struggling with a particularly difficult crossword, dear
heart ...
Charlie He knows what I'm talking about. One day a lengthy lecture on my
morals and less than a week later I find ——
Ben Oh, do go on — I'm sure we're all agog ...
Charlie (*turning away*) Oh, piss off ...!

Sam enters determined to do something positive

Sam Just look at you all. What the hell is going on? I thought we had a
problem here. Is no-one even going to try to sort it out?
Richard Quite right, Sam. I think we should all go indoors, open the
champagne and leave Ben and your mother here to have a chat. (*He rises*)
Charlie I'm buggered if I'm moving just to please him.
Jan Your father's right. I think Ben has a little explaining to do. He got us
into this mess.
Charlie If you think I'm going to be ordered about by this creep ...

Jan Charles! I shall not ask you again. Go. Now.
Sam Well, if you want my opinion ——
Jan We don't.
Sam Why is it this family can never get together without having a row ...?

Sam and Charlie exit indoors

Richard Good luck, dear. Call if I'm needed. (*He tries to lighten the atmosphere*) Perhaps I'll have a go on my contraption — what do you think?

Jan glares at Richard

Knowing it best not to argue, Richard exits into the house

Silence

Jan looks across at Ben. He looks across at her. She turns away. He takes an apple from the bowl on the table, sits at the table, and bites into the apple

Ben (*at length*) Sam tells me Dad's lost all his money. Four years ago. Is that right?
Jan Trust her to tell you that!
Ben Bit headstrong, wasn't it?
Jan He was hoping to secure my future.

Ben laughs

It was a risk — a risk which didn't pay off. We don't all have your Midas touch.
Ben And now you've gone and sold his movie collection. Why? I've told you umpteen times: if you're short of money ——
Jan You still think signing a cheque puts everything right, don't you?
Ben How will you manage?
Jan We shall. We always have. (*Beat*) Well ...?
Ben What ...?
Jan Why the hell didn't you tell me you were bringing *him* here?
Ben (*amused*) You're angry. I can tell. You're seething with it. Nice apples.
Jan Next time round I'm going to have dogs instead of children. At least from a dog one can expect loyalty and devotion.
Ben I'll get you a dog if you want one.
Jan (*turning on him*) I'm going to hit you, Ben — I'm warning you! (*Almost breathless with anger, she tries to calm herself*) "Richard's seventieth," I

thought, "we'll do something special, bless him ... A party," I thought, "here in the garden ... I'll invite the kids: moody Charles; unlucky Sam; darling Ben ... We shall have to put up with Hettie, I thought, but we shall cope with that ... Phone calls were made, invitations accepted, and that, or so I foolishly imagined, was that ... The sun will shine, the birds will sing, the champagne will flow — and all will be well. (*She turns and glares at Ben*) And it had to be you, hadn't it? It had to be Ben who decides to put the mockers on it all. Yes, dear, I am angry — bloody angry, in fact!

Ben You see? I was right.

Jan And if you must know, your father has already forgiven me for selling his collection, so it has nothing whatsoever to do with you, or Sam, or Charlie — right?

Ben Is that it? Is the performance over?

Jan No, there's one more thing. Are you homosexual or not? And if so, why was I never informed?

Ben (*laughing*) Oh, that's a new one — well done, Mother.

Jan (*sitting*) Not that it matters a jot any longer. Nothing could shock me more than your extraordinary behaviour this afternoon.

Ben I've said I'm sorry.

Jan Where did you find that man? Scoured every beach bar and gambling den on both sides of the equator, I suppose.

Ben I tried to tell you all this earlier but you were in no mood to listen. He found me, if you must know.

Jan Now why doesn't that surprise me? Short of cash, was he?

Ben Are you going to listen or not?

Jan looks away

He found me. He wrote to me. At the office. Said he was back in England for a while but made it quite clear in his letter that if I had no desire to get in touch with him — fine. No hard feelings.

Jan looks across at Ben in disbelief

I wrote back.

Jan You wrote back. I see. How cosy. Go on.

Ben I met him a couple of times and I liked him. I'm sorry — but I did. In fact, the more I saw him the more I liked him. I suggested he came down here with me today. Just to meet us all again. That's about it.

Jan "Daddy, Daddy!" you cried, "Fate has brought us together again after all these years!"

Ben (*rising as if to go*) Oh well, if you're going to send the whole thing up. (*He throws his apple core away*)

Jan No, please continue: it's breaking my heart.

Ben I honestly, hand on heart, thought you'd like to meet him again, settle old scores, catch up with each other's past. You're not going to deny you've often wondered what became of him. You loved the guy once.

Jan Yes, *once*, a lifetime ago: not any more.

Ben At least you can talk to him. Ask why he walked out on us.

Jan I know why he walked out on us.

Ben I don't. Charlie doesn't. Nor does Sam.

Jan It's none of your business.

Ben (*hurt*) Oh, thanks. None of our business.

Jan You know what I mean. He left because he couldn't handle the responsibility, Ben. Our marriage was fine until you three came along.

Ben So it's all our fault ...?

Jan Of course not. All I'm saying is — our life changed. He had to knuckle under, settle down, find a job, a job he could hang on to. Bringing him here today was selfish and irresponsible of you. How do you think your father feels ...?

Ben Richard's fine. I've talked to him. He's just as intrigued by all this as I am. He knows Brice poses no threat to your marriage — he makes not the slightest difference.

Jan So why in the name of all that's wonderful did you bring him here?

Ben Because you could be friends. Isn't that possible? He's our dad — and Richard isn't going to last forever.

Jan (*hurt, furiously*) Don't say that! Don't you dare say that!

Ben (*angry with himself now*) I'm sorry, I'm sorry. I was out of order; I didn't think.

Jan Liar! You always think. You think too much, that's your problem. And, God forgive me for saying it, you have a malicious streak in you, Ben — you always have had. You knew fetching Brice here today would cause one almighty row and for some obscure reason that amused you.

Ben All right, so you want the truth. What if I've just grown tired of all this pretence?

Jan What pretence?

Ben Your world of pretence. Everything perfect: perfect children, perfect marriage, like an old black-and-white movie.

Jan What's wrong with that?

Ben It's a façade, Mother. Make-believe. We aren't perfect. I'm only happy when I'm making money which is why I never stop working. Charlie and Sam have miserable marriages.

Jan That is not true: Charlie and Kay are very happy.

Ben Oh yes? Since when? Look, Mum, Richard's a great guy, a lovely guy — but he's our stepfather. Why do we have to pretend he's our father?

Jan (*trying to defend herself*) I don't pretend — I just want ...

Ben What, Mother? What do you want? Happy-ever-after? Is that it? And
if we haven't got happy-ever-after we're failures?
Jan Of course not ... I simply want everyone to ——
Ben Don't say it. Is Charlie happy? Sam? Me? Are you?

Jan looks at Ben

Life isn't all wonderful, Mum. Things go wrong, people cock up, relation-
ships fail — we fail.
Jan I know that. I know life can sometimes deal us a rough hand, but I won't
have you saying we're all failures — I won't have that.
Ben You brought us up to expect perfection and nothing else. You tried to
create a world of illusion where nothing could possibly go wrong. The
result is: we can't cope with our own short-comings, let alone each other's.
Jan (*rising*) I see. Suddenly it's me who's in the wrong. Well, of course. It's
a mother's place to be in the wrong. However hard you try, when they grow
up your kids believe you got it wrong. If I tried to make you believe that
you could *be* anything you liked, *do* anything you liked, if I tried to teach
you independence and self-reliance — was that so wrong?
Ben You know what's sad? You refuse to face reality and you don't even
know you're doing it. Maybe, by bringing him here today, I wanted, just
once, to make you face up to the truth.
Jan Well, you've certainly done that, Ben. Congratulations!

Brice appears at the back gate

(*Turning and seeing Brice*) Oh ...
Brice (*aware of the atmosphere*) It's nice. The bay and everything. Fresh air,
sea breezes. You did well for yourself, Jan.
Ben (*turning to go indoors*) I'm in need of a drink.
Jan Ben ... no.
Ben Time's running out, Mother. We have to be back in London by tonight.

Ben exits

Jan, feeling awkward, sits on a bench at the table, refusing to look at Brice.
Brice never takes his eyes off Jan

Brice (*at length*) You haven't changed at all. You look as young as ever.
Jan Oh, please — spare me that.
Brice (*coming* DS, *looking out to sea*) The sea's bluer than I'd imagined. It's
almost Mediterranean.
Jan Well, it isn't. It's Freshwater Bay and you've chosen a nice day. Well,
a nice day for some things.

Brice (*rolling another cigarette*) I didn't want to come. Ben persuaded me. "It'll be an adventure," he said. You know me — I could never resist an adventure. (*Beat*) It must be bleak in winter.

Jan It is. But at least then it's ours. We've come to dislike the summer. It brings unwelcome strangers. (*Beat*) I see you still smoke those nasty things.

Brice Yes. I have tried to give them up. Didn't know what to do with my hands. (*He moves to a seat*) May I?

Jan I'd rather you didn't make yourself too comfortable.

Brice (*sitting*) Richard seems a delightful chap.

Jan He is. Very delightful. Very loyal. Very dependable. The total opposite of you.

Brice I hadn't realized he was that much older than you. Pity about Sam's boy. What is it?

Jan Autism. But he's become very precious to us all. (*Beat*) What's behind all this?

Brice All what?

Jan You're not expecting me to believe you just dropped in for tea. How did you find Ben?

Brice I was given his address by mutual friends.

Jan We have no mutual friends. I haven't set eyes on you for over thirty years.

Brice Very *old* mutual friends.

Jan (*still not looking at Brice at all*) I see. Rose and Barnaby.

Brice With whom I always kept in touch. But then you know that.

Jan Just how much have you told Ben?

Brice Very little. It's obvious he thinks I'm the bad guy in all this.

Jan And you don't?

Brice Highly dangerous. Believing one's own lies.

Jan I haven't lied. Embroidered the facts slightly. I don't call that lying.

Ben enters from the house carrying a glass of wine and a can of beer

Ben I thought this might help. Make your journey into the past more palatable. (*He gives the wine to Jan*) I'm relieved you haven't killed him yet. (*He gives the beer to Brice*) Everything OK?

Brice We're managing, thank you. Just about. Cheers.

Ben I'm trying to organize party games in there so the atmosphere's ever so gay. (*He laughs*) Did she tell you she accused me of being a raging puff earlier?

Brice And are you?

Ben Ahh ... Other people's sex lives can be deeply intriguing, can't they? (*He heads back indoors*) Just scream if you need help.

Ben exits

Brice He's OK. I like him more and more.
Jan He's been spoiled.
Brice What about Sam? Is she happily married?
Jan She's married—but not happily. Her husband is a philanderer, a wastrel and a good-for-nothing. Sound familiar? He's also never forgiven her for giving birth to a child he regards as incomplete.
Brice I was never a philanderer.
Jan Two out of three isn't bad. I take it you never remarried.
Brice Why would I? I made a complete mess of the first one. (*Beat*) Tell me about Charlie.
Jan He tells us nothing. But from what I've heard today he and his wife are never likely to become Darby and Joan. All sounds a bit of a mess, doesn't it?
Brice For which you blame me I suppose.
Jan For good or ill, Brice, you were never around for long enough to make any impression on my children. And their upbringing in this house was blissfully peaceful and happy. Richard saw to that.
Brice Always away a lot, Ben said. Months on end sometimes. It seems to have been your destiny to lead a solitary life. (*He rises to find an ashtray*)
Jan One can hardly be solitary with three growing kids to bring up.
Brice We have four grandchildren he tells me.
Jan We? *I* have four grandchildren. You can lay no claim to them.
Brice (*sitting beside Jan*) You're still as beautiful as ever. Does Richard tell you that?
Jan All the time.
Brice And you love him?
Jan I adore him.

Brice touches Jan's hair, an intimate reminder of their past

Brice (*lowering his voice*) Does he make your toes curl?

Jan moves away slightly. The air is heavy with things remembered

He's rather unwell, Ben tells me.
Jan He *was* unwell. He's completely recovered now.
Brice (*softly*) I never stopped loving you, Jan.

This is now too uncomfortable for Jan. She rises and moves DS

Jan (*perhaps to change the subject*) You need a haircut. And a shave. You always were untidy. At least you got rid of that dreadful pony-tail.

Brice (*rising and standing behind her again*) Come on — you loved my
   pony-tail. Hair cascading all over the pillow, you thrashing about on top of
   me ...

Jan Stop it. Someone may hear.

Brice What is it they say? You always remember your first.

Jan I wasn't your first — or your twenty-first come to that.

Brice I meant you. I was your first. A shy, timid little virgin who turned into
   a ——

Jan Please ...

Brice Those endless nights in bed, watching the rain beating at the
   windows ...

Jan (*moving away* C) I'm going in ...

Brice OK, I give in: pax. You needn't be scared.

Jan (*laughing*) Scared? Of you? Some things are best forgotten — that's all.

Brice (*sitting at the table again*) OK, what *shall* we talk about?

Jan I would simply prefer it if you left — now.

Brice What, and come all this way, after all these years — for nothing.
   There's stuff I want to know, Jan.

Jan Such as what?

Brice (*looking at Jan*) Why?

Jan (*sitting on the lounger*) You know why. I did what I thought was right
   — at least what I thought was right at the time.

Brice You always were such a high-principled little madam. Busily trying
   to make me into Mr-Nine-to-Five. Couldn't you see that was impossible?

Jan For the sake of the kids, I saw no harm in trying.

Brice And eventually you got one; is that what you wanted?

Jan Richard was never a nine-to-five man.

Brice But he was safe. Predictable. What was it you said? Loyal —
   dependable — solid as a rock.

Jan That's nothing to sneer at.

Brice Who's sneering? I merely asked if he turned out to be what you wanted.

Jan Yes. Very much so — and more. Look, Brice, we could never have
   worked. I couldn't live the life you wanted. Never any money for bills,
   forever behind with the rent, struggling to feed the kids for God's sake.
   What sort of life is that?

Brice You're saying things improved when I left?

Jan No, I'm not. But at least the responsibility was mine. At least I had to
   do something instead of living on empty promises.

Brice It wasn't all bad. There were some good things.

Jan What? The sex? Another child every year? I was twenty years old, Brice.

Brice So was I.

Jan Oh, come off it. You were never twenty years old. It was like having yet
   another child in the house.

Brice (*amused*) I'm sorry.
Jan Don't be sorry. Just forget it ever happened. I have.
Brice Have you? Can you honestly say you've never even thought of me all this time?
Jan Only every time I received another of your bloody letters.
Brice And in between.

There is a pause

Jan (*softening slightly*) All right ... sometimes in between.
Brice What we had was once-in-a-lifetime stuff.
Jan But it wasn't enough, can't you see that? Can't you get that into your head ...?

Brice rises and re-lights his cigarette

Jan I hope that *is* tobacco you're smoking!

There is a pause

Brice After I left ... how did you manage? (*He moves to Jan's chair, ashtray in hand, and sits on the ground at her feet*)
Jan (*almost amused to remember*) I've no idea. But I did. Two endless years of cleaning houses, offices; waiting at tables; and any other underpaid work I could find. Eventually, through a friend of mine, I got some work as a film extra. That's how I met Richard.
Brice It didn't matter that he was older?
Jan No. Why should it? Anyway, he didn't look forty. I fell in love with him the moment I saw him. He was kind, funny, charming and the perfect gentleman at all times. He courted me, sent me flowers, took me to the cinema, out for meals. It was months before we went to bed, if that's what you're thinking.
Brice It wasn't.
Jan Finally, he asked us to move in with him. He always loved the kids and they adored him. Then, after I'd divorced you, we married, came over here, saw this house, bought it — and we've lived happily ever after.

Beat

I hate myself for asking this — but did you ever miss us at all?
Brice You know I did. (*Beat*) Why did you never answer any of my letters?
Jan Did you expect me to? Anyway, you were always so constantly on the move, how was I to know you'd receive them?

Brice Rose and Barnaby always knew where I was. You could have used the same arrangement: sent your replies to them and they'd have passed them on.

Jan Yes, well, it's too late now.

Brice Not everything's too late, Jan.

Jan Isn't it? (*Beat*) You still haven't answered my question.

Brice Why did I come back? Maybe I was curious to see you all again, see how things had turned out. But, don't worry, I'm happy to go on my way. I'm a travelling man; another town, another country.

Jan Another woman.

Brice That was never our problem and you know it. Other women only became necessary after you didn't want me.

Jan I never said I didn't want you. I couldn't live with you, that's all.

Brice (*taking her hand*) Do you still want me?

Jan I just wish to God you'd never come here. (*She tries to free her hand from his*) Brice — please.

Brice Go on, say it: you've never stopped wanting me, have you?

Jan I shall call for someone ...

Brice I want to know why you let me go ...

Jan And I've told you: you needed freedom and I wanted security. You couldn't offer that. Now let go of me ... (*She wrenches her hand free, rises and moves away*)

Brice (*getting to his feet*) Coward.

Jan Just go — please go.

Brice Not until you tell me you have no regrets.

Jan I haven't ... None ... Ever.

Brice And that you're happy.

Jan I am. You can see I am. I'm tired of this, Brice. Please leave us alone.

Brice Did Richard ever know about my letters?

Jan Of course not. And he must never know. Nor must the kids.

Brice Poor Jan. Never mind. (*Beat*) It's odd. Seeing you again. Ben was right; you haven't changed at all. I still pictured you in that squalid little flat, ironing, preparing meals; or, once the kids were in bed, you and me snuggled up in front of that old gas fire. (*Beat. He moves towards Jan*) You're not going to believe this, but there hasn't been a day when I haven't thought of you. (*He stands just behind her and almost whispers*) I still love you.

There is silence now — just the distant sounds of the sea and seagulls can be heard

Jan What was the real reason for coming back? Just tell me the truth.

Brice The truth. Do any of us ever speak the truth?

Jan Strangely enough most of us do. You're the only person who ever made a liar of me.

Brice If you really want to know — I came back to see Barnaby. He's dying.

Jan (*deeply shocked*) I didn't know that. Why didn't Rose tell me?

Brice She felt she couldn't. She knew about Richard's heart attack and thought you had enough worries of your own. I needed to know you were safe.

Jan Safe ...?

Brice You know what I mean. I needed to know that the world you created for yourself was secure.

Jan I don't understand you.

Brice No. You never did. You're my wife, Jan.

Jan (*moving away from Brice again*) I am *not* your wife. We're divorced.

Brice You think that matters? To me you'll always be my wife.

Jan I don't trust you, Brice, I'm sorry. Could it be that you thought Richard was terminally ill and that you could step into his shoes ...?

Brice That's unfair.

Jan Tired of your aimless existence, are you? Ready to settle down; a free meal-ticket courtesy of your rich son, a ready-made home with no responsibilities? You disgust me!

Brice (*hurt*) How eager you are to think badly of me. I came here today because I thought you might need me.

Jan Even if the worst had happened, whatever made you think I'd need you of all people?

Brice (*taking her by the shoulders*) I simply wanted you to know that I'll always be here for you. Any time, any place, for the rest of my life.

Jan Pity you weren't there when we had three young children to support.

Brice Oh, I was there for you, Jan — it was you who wasn't there for me ...

There is a sudden commotion in the house; the sound of raised voices

Richard (*off*) Please, Hettie — let's not have all this, today of all days ...

Hettie (*off*) I know it's none of my business, Richard, but enough is enough ....

Jan (*quickly moving away from Brice*) Oh, God — it's Hettie again ...

Hettie, dressed for a journey and carrying a small suitcase, a headscarf and a pair of gloves, comes storming out of the house

Richard follows Hettie out

During the following, Ben, Charlie and Sam come out one by one to watch the ensuing drama from the terrace

Hettie (*half in anger, half in drink*) I'm sorry, Janet, but I can remain in this house no longer ...
Jan What have we done now ....?
Hettie Thank you for putting up with me, but I shall sponge off you no more ...
Richard Hettie, this is simply ridiculous ... !
Sam Oh, just let her go, Dad.
Richard Keep out of this, all of you ....
Hettie (*putting on the headscarf and gloves*) I've been watching you from my window, Janet. Laughing, joking, flirting with this ... This....
Jan I have not been flirting, or laughing or joking. Richard, I swear we haven't. Brice, have we been ...?
Hettie And I saw him trying to kiss you.
Jan You're talking absolute rubbish ....
Hettie Yes, well that's all I ever do, isn't it? You snigger behind my back, your children make fun of me ——
Ben What have we said now ... ?
Richard Ben — shut up!
Hettie I'm sorry I ever came to the island in the first place ...
Charlie (*about Brice*) This is all his fault ...
Hettie Of course, knowing Janet's weakness for lame dogs, the next thing we can expect is he'll be living here. A cosy ménage à trois I suppose. And you, Richard, being the fool you are, will allow it to happen. Well, I'm sorry, but I refuse to live in a house where morals and human dignity have no meaning ...
Jan Please, Hettie — for Richard's sake ...
Hettie I shall go to my sister in Worthing. At least there I shall be made to feel welcome. (*She heads for the back gate*) And have no fear — I shall not return this time. Consider me gone. And, for all you care, gone to my grave ...!

Hettie exits through the gate

Richard (*calling after Hettie*) I am not coming looking for you this time, Hettie — I swear to God I'm not! (*He closes the gate*)

There is an embarrassed silence for a moment

Richard I really do apologize, old boy. Rather highly strung, I'm afraid.
Charlie Highly pissed you mean.
Jan Charles! That's enough!

Charlie, Ben and Sam sit down

Brice I hope none of this is my fault.

Richard Not at all. It happens quite regularly. (*He sits*)
Jan (*putting a hand on Richard's shoulder*) Don't worry, darling. We'll give
her till dusk then we'll go down and fetch her.
Ben (*amused*) From where?
Richard She sits in a disused bus shelter down by the beach waiting for a
bus she knows will never come. I'm afraid all this excitement has been too
much for her.
Charlie Excitement? Where?

Jan glares at him

OK, when's he leaving? Because if he's not — we are. Sam?
Sam I'm going nowhere until we hear what he has to say for himself.
Richard Manners, Sam. This gentleman is your father and he does have a
name. (*To Brice*) You're welcome to stay as long as you wish. And that
applies to you all. The celebrations aren't over yet.

An awkward pause

Right, what do we do next? Pass the parcel? (*He laughs*)

No-one else laughs

*Eunice appears at the back gate, all smiles as usual and having changed
her dress again*

Eunice Co-ee! It's only me. I see Hettie's off again with her little suitcase.
Jan You've changed again.
Eunice (*obviously out to attract Brice*) You know me — I dress to suit my
mood. Things still a bit dicey are they?
Charlie He's still here if that's what you mean.
Jan I hope we didn't drive you away.
Eunice Not at all. I've weathered worse storms than this, I can tell you. So
tell us, Brice — what do you think of the island?
Brice From the little I've seen — it's beautiful.
Ben (*his attempt at a joke*) Fancy living here?
Jan (*warningly*) Ben ...!
Richard And our house — you like our house, I'm sure.
Brice Very much. May I ask why the room you call the den is so modern
when the rest of the house is so ...
Richard Scruffy? Ramshackle? Ah well, you'll have to ask my wife. I'm
afraid she's in the dog house.
Eunice Don't tease her now, please.
Jan Don't worry; I'm never going to be allowed to forget it. (*To Brice*) It used
to house Richard's rare and wonderful collection of film memorabilia. But
I got rid of it.

Sam Go on; tell the truth.

Richard Sam — please ...

Jan (*still ashamed*) I sold it. We did need the money.

Ben Who the hell did you sell it to? I can't imagine anyone wanting all that old junk.

Sam hits out at Ben. Ben playfully puts up his hands to shield himself

Jan A little man in Ventnor who shares your father's passion for old movies. He was very nice.

Richard He must have come when I wasn't here.

Jan He did. You went up to London for the day. It was very convenient. That's when Mr Quincey called to collect the stuff.

Sam "Stuff!" Can you hear this, Dad?

Richard Well, if Mr Quincey derives only half the pleasure I did from the collection then I'm delighted. Now, indoors, all of you. We'll cut the cake, open my presents, and get roaring drunk. (*To Brice*) You will join us?

Brice I'd love to.

Richard Splendid, old boy. Right, come along, I'm in charge from now on.

All except Jan, Ben and Brice make their way indoors

Eunice (*linking her arm with Richard's*) The champagne should be just right. And please, Richard, could we have some music? It is supposed to be a party.

Richard (*as they go inside*) As long as it's my kind of music ...

All except Jan, Brice and Ben exit

Ben I need to make a phone call, Mum.

Jan Use the one in our bedroom if it's private.

Ben follows the others indoors

Brice Does this mean I've been accepted?

Jan I wouldn't bank on it. Moods in this house can change with the wind.

Brice I thought you said you were happy.

Jan I am.

Brice Still scrimping and scraping by the sound of it. Just like the old days. Life turned full circle, has it?

Jan just looks at Brice

Coming in?

Jan Shortly. I need a moment to myself.

We hear music coming from the house; a popular tune from the sixties

Brice heads indoors

Miles enters from the house and stands staring at Brice, his face quite expressionless

Brice seems a little unnerved by Miles for a second

Brice exits

Miles goes over to Jan

Jan Hallo, darling. (*She takes his hand*) You all right?
Miles Cards ...?
Jan Not just now, love. Nan's quite exhausted.

Jan puts an arm around Miles and draws him close to her

Miles (*about the music*) Happy birthday ...?
Jan Yes, love. Happy birthday. Oh, I hope to God life is different for you ...

The music grows louder, filling the auditorium. The Lights slowly fade

We move as swiftly as possible into the last scene

Charlie, Sam, Ben, Brice, Eunice and Richard join Jan and Miles on stage

Miles lies on the lounger, fast asleep, with Charlie, without his shoes, asleep on the ground beside him. The rest are dancing, Sam with Ben, Brice with Eunice, Richard with Jan

The Lights come up. It is evening. Lights from the house and from the terrace create shadows over everything; things have taken on quite a romantic air. Empty wine bottles, glasses etc. litter the table

The music changes: Manfred Mann sings "Pretty Flamingo". There are lots of laughter, chatter and singing as they join in the song

Eunice (*the worse for drink*) This man dances like a dream, Jan.
Jan Yes, but be careful — he'll dance you to heaven knows where.
Richard This song means a lot to your mother and me. Remember, darling?
Jan I do. The Dorchester — the BAFTAs.

Jan and Richard dance closer now, both with their eyes closed

Ben (*to Sam as they dance*) Charlie looks done in.
Sam Pissed. I can see I'll have to do the driving tonight. My son's well away too. He can sleep through anything.

Charlie struggles to his feet and makes his way to the table for another drink

Jan Stop him, Richard. He's had far too much.
Richard (*going to Charlie*) Come along, old boy. Black coffee for you now.
Charlie I'm OK, mate ... I'm fine ... I'm OK.
Jan Only if you promise to stay the night, Charlie.
Charlie (*leaning on the table*) I don't want to stay the night. Not with him around.
Brice (*dancing with Eunice*) Don't worry, Charlie — I shall be going back to my lonely little bedsitter in Hammersmith.
Eunice Oh, what a pity. Must you? You could always stay at my place, Brice.

The rest make the appropriate sounds for when sex is in the air

The music suddenly stops. Everyone moans

Sam What's happened to the music ....?
Jan (*already knowing the cause*) Oh, Lord, brace yourselves — she's back!

Hettie enters from the house

Hettie You can hear that din half way down the street! We'll have the police here next!
Richard Hettie, my love, thank God: we were worried out of our wits about you!
Hettie They've obviously cancelled the bus. I shall have to go to Worthing tomorrow. Now, if we might have less noise I shall go to bed and try to sleep.
Ben (*stirring it*) I could drive you to Worthing, Hettie — I don't mind.
Jan Ben! Stop it!
Hettie No, thank you. If I go — when I go — I shall go under my own steam.

Hettie exits

Richard Oh dear. Well, that's it, folks — talk in whispers from now on.

They all find seats in various parts of the garden, Eunice sticking close to Brice

Sam It's beyond me why you put up with her at all.

Jan Because she's your father's sister. Although why she persists in doing this to herself ... She always has to face the humiliation of coming back.

Brice What's the fascination with Worthing?

Eunice She has a sister there, apparently.

Richard We have no sister in Worthing. We have no sister anywhere. We did have — but she died many years ago.

Sam You never told us that.

Richard No, well, we all have our pretty secrets, our family skeletons. If it keeps her happy to fantasize ...

Eunice What about her husband — did he exist?

Richard Oh, indeed. The once Very Reverend Samuel Popplewell. A parson who committed some unspoken misdemeanour and was obliged to leave the church under a cloud.

Eunice (*quite moved*) Oh, dear — poor Hettie.

Richard The least Jan and I can do is see she comes to no harm. Right, what shall we do now? Blindman's Buff ...?

Eunice Oh, yes, please — and I shall be blindfolded.

Jan You're going to regret this in the morning, Eunice.

Eunice I know — isn't it fun?

Charlie (*jumping to his feet, unsteady*) I know — we could play "Guess-the-Movie".

All the family moan

What's wrong with "Guess-the-Movie" ...?

Eunice What is it?

Jan We played it all the time when they were kids.

Richard Movies have played a very important part in our lives, Brice. These kids know just about every good movie ever made.

Ben And plenty of bad ones.

Brice Count me out; I'm not very good at games.

Eunice Nor me. I never went to the pictures. I was into dancing. What were you into, Brice?

Charlie Come on, then; I'll start us off.

Sam Oh, sit down, Charlie.

Richard Leave him, he's happy.

Charlie (*taking centre stage*) Right, no words — OK?

Richard Ah, the boy's a mime artiste!

Charlie enacts the shower scene from "Psycho", first taking off a set of female clothes, then stepping "naked" into a shower, turning on the hot water and allowing it to splash over his face

Richard Look out — here comes Old Mother Bates.

Charlie goes into the famous screeching sound, using an imaginary knife to make violent stabbing movements. He is backed up by the rest of the family joining in. The family, well impressed and applauding, cry out "Psycho — Psycho — Oscar — Oscar!" etc. Charlie, almost child-like, seems well pleased with his efforts

Eunice Well, everyone knows that one ...!
Jan (*laughing*) That's the whole point of the game, Eunice.
Eunice (*blankly*) Oh, I see ....
Richard Come on, Sam — do your favourite.

Sam, also childishly excited, gets up and "gets into character"

Sam Music, please — I must have the music.

The family, together, start to hum the theme from "Gone with the Wind" as Sam becomes Scarlett O'Hara, the wind blowing in her face as she looks out, wipes her face, then bends down and pulls an imaginary turnip from the ground. She holds it up and takes a deep breath

(*In a Deep South accent*) "As God is my witness — I shall never go hungry again ...!"

The humming swells; they applaud her

All *Gone With the Wind* ...! Well done! (*Etc., etc.*)
Brice The only film quote I know is: "Frankly, my dear, I don't give a damn!"
Sam (*returning to her seat*) How very appropriate.
Charlie Me again —— (*He rises and starts to prepare*)
Richard Now, now, Charlie, one go at a time — them's the rules.
Ben Ah, leave him — he can have my go.
Jan That's very nice of you, Ben.
Ben Well, I am nice, Mum — aren't I ... ?
Charlie Right, ready; who's this? (*He goes into his James Cagney routine*) "I'm on top of the world, Ma; Ma, I'm on top of the world ... Ma, I'm on top ..."
Sam OK, OK ... You're on top of the world. We get the picture — now sit down.
Charlie (*grinning*) It's James Cagney, "you dirty rats!"
Eunice I read somewhere that he never actually said "You dirty rat". I liked him best in *Love Me Or Leave Me* with Doris Day. (*To Brice*) I always wanted to be Doris Day — so wholesome, so nice ...

Richard "I knew Doris Day before she was a virgin ...!"
Charlie (*to Eunice; out of control now*) You look nothing like Doris Day, you stupid cow!
Jan (*horrified*) Charles!

There is a dreadful silence

Charlie (*dazed, muttering*) She looks nothing like ——
Richard That's enough, Charlie. That is no way to speak to a guest!
Jan I'm so sorry, Eunice ...
Eunice Oh, not to worry; we're all a bit the worse for drink. (*She rises*) Look, shall I make us all some coffee — how's that?
Jan You can't keep doing everything.
Eunice Oh, yes I can. (*She moves rather unsteadily towards the house*) Shall I pop up and say hallo to you-know-who?
Jan Would you? It might just do the trick.

Eunice goes into the house

Ben helps himself to more wine at the table. Charlie slumps down by him

Ben You can be a right prick at times, can't you.
Charlie Sod off.

Miles wakes up, unsure where he is

Miles (*rubbing his eyes*) Mum ... Mum ...?
Sam It's all right, darling — I'm here. (*To Jan*) Can I put him to bed in your room till we leave?
Jan Of course. Quieter upstairs, eh, Miles?

Sam leads Miles off into the house

Everyone is silent

Richard I'm sure we're all very tired. That's what it is. (*He yawns and stretches*) Still, on the whole, I think it's been a wonderful day — all in all.
Charlie Oh, you do, do you, old chap. All in all and all that.
Jan Charlie, not now, please.
Charlie Oh, yes, I forgot: must keep quiet, keep your mouth shut, Charlie, keep up the pretence, don't rattle the cage. Well, now it's my turn to upset the family apple-cart ...
Richard (*to heaven*) Oh, God ...

Charlie I would like to make an announcement. I would like it known that, come September, I shall be leaving my wife and children.
Jan (*stunned*) Is he serious?
Ben Oh, shut up; no-one cares anyway.
Charlie Oh, no — no-one cares what I do. Of course if little Ben announced he was leaving his boyfriend ——
Ben Just ignore him. I do.
Charlie — or even if he'd ever had the guts to come out and admit what he was — even to himself.
Ben You're a pathetic, whinging little piss-artist. My life, just like yours, is of no interest to anyone here — so stuff it!
Richard (*with unexpected force and anger*) Stop it! Both of you! We're sick and tired of all this. How you choose to run your private lives is of no concern to us — right?
Ben What I said exactly.
Richard Ben, I mean it. Stop all this bloody foolish bickering. (*He reacts to a sudden pain in his chest*)

Jan looks anxious

Richard (*rising*) I'm going in — I think I'm in need of one of my tablets.
Jan (*rising*) Richard ...
Richard (*moving towards the house*) I'm OK, Jan. I'm OK, dear.

Richard exits

Jan (*moving to the terrace*) Now see what you've done. Can't you see he's not well?
Ben Shall I go to him?
Jan Stay where you are. I want to hear this. Now, Charlie, could you tell us, quite calmly, what all this is about?
Charlie I hate her; that's all. We hate each other. Our marriage is a disaster so I'm doing what he did: I'm getting out of it, leaving home.
Jan Ben — did you know about this?
Ben Don't drag me into it — I couldn't care less.
Jan Answer me. Did you know?
Ben That he had another woman? Yes. He came to me expecting some brotherly sympathy and understanding. All he got was a pep talk on his obligations to his children — but I needn't have bothered, it fell on stony ground. A week later he burst into my office, caused an embarrassing scene in front of my staff and generally made a prat of himself. Made unpleasant accusations about me and a guy I happen to share a house with and ——
Charlie He's your lover, for Christ's sake — just admit it ...

Ben He has some little tart in tow. She's known as the airport bike; she thinks because he's my brother he must be loaded.

Charlie (*trying to stand*) She is not after my money.

Ben You haven't got any money, Charlie. In fact, you're up to your eyeballs in debt — spent mostly on a pathetic scrubber who's been through half of Heathrow.

Charlie (*taking a swipe at Ben*) Liar ... !

Brice jumps up to restrain Charlie

Sam appears on the terrace

Brice (*grabbing Charlie by the waist*) That's enough now, Charlie ...

Ben (*ready for a fight*) Come on, hit me; that's just about your mark ...

Brice Just calm down, Ben — leave it, please.

Charlie (*trying to free himself from Brice*) Piss off, you! Get back to wherever it is you came from ... ! (*Suddenly, he feels sick and saliva drips from his mouth; he becomes almost child-like*)

Jan (*distraught*) I don't believe this is happening.

Brice steers the weeping Charlie towards a table bench

Brice Come on, let's have you sitting down.

Sam What's brought all this on?

Jan goes over to Charlie, pushes Brice aside and sits, her arms around her son

Jan I'll see to him.

Charlie (*crying like a baby*) I'm sorry, Mum ...

Jan Shh, shh, now ...

Charlie I went to him for help ... Who else had I? I was in debt, behind with my mortgage — he promised to lend me some money.

Ben Tell the truth, why can't you? I said I'd pay off all his debts only on condition that he dropped his little tart who'd caused all his problems in the first place, pulled himself together and tried to make a go of it with Kay for the sake of the kids. It was you who made a promise, Charlie.

Charlie You have no right to tell me how to run my life.

Ben Oh, no? You're a loser, Charlie; you always have been.

Jan (*cradling Charlie in her arms*) That's enough now, Ben.

Ben Yes, well, as long as we're all quite clear about this. It's not me who's the bastard round here.

Brice Yes, OK, Ben — we get the picture.

Ben sits, exhausted. Charlie puts his feet up on the bench and curls up in his mother's lap. During the following he falls asleep

Sam I think it's time I got him home, don't you?
Jan He'll be fine.

Sam goes US *and lights a cigarette*

Brice Isn't it time we were off, Ben?
Sam Oh, great; now he wants to disappear again. See what you've started? Happy families, is this.
Ben (*rising, making to leave*) Want to go? I'm willing.
Jan Ben, don't. It's Richard's party.
Ben Some party — what?

  Richard appears on the terrace

Richard I apologize. I behaved disgracefully. (*Beat*) Eunice wants to know how many for coffee.

No-one answers

(*Sitting*) As you so rightly say, Ben — some party.

Silence

Brice (*at length*) Look, before I go, and as we appear to be clearing the air ——
Jan (*warily*) Not now, Brice.
Brice I'd rather get this over and done with, then I can make my way back to London. (*He moves to Richard*) I owe you an apology, Richard. I had no business coming here today.
Richard My dear chap ...
Brice It was thoughtless and inexcusable. I had no right to intrude on a family party.
Ben You are family.
Brice No. I forfeited that right the day I walked out. I can only thank you for being a wonderful replacement, far more reliable than the original.
Richard Good God, man, I wouldn't even presume to think that.
Brice I couldn't have left my children in better hands.
Sam But you didn't know that at the time, did you? And obviously you couldn't have cared less.
Richard Now, Sam ——

Sam No, I'm sorry, Dad — someone has to say it. (*To Brice*) I suppose you thought that by turning up here today you'd be forgiven for what you did to us. Well, not as far as I'm concerned. Have you even the remotest idea what effect it had on Mum?

Jan (*quietly*) Don't be silly; you were far too young, Sam.

Sam He very nearly ruined our lives, Mother.

Richard (*hurt*) Thank you.

Sam All right, Dad, so we were lucky — you came along, thank God — but for all he knew we could have been out on the street starving to death.

Richard You're being melodramatic; you survived.

Sam I don't understand you, Dad. Or Mum. He's just being allowed to get away with what he did.

Richard It was all a lifetime ago, Sam; none of it matters any more.

Silence. Sam knows she's wasting her breath. She sits at the table

There is a pause

Jan He did know.

Sam Sorry ...?

Jan Brice did know what had happened to us.

Brice Come on, Ben — it's time we were going.

Ben Hang on. What are you saying, Mother?

Jan He always knew we were safe and well. And he knew I'd married Richard.

Brice Jan, there's no need.

Jan I think there's every need. And he kept in touch. For the first few years anyway.

Sam I don't understand ...

Jan Our friends, Rose and Barnaby; Brice sent his letters to them, they in turn passed them on to me. He always remembered each of your birthdays and always sent his love. (*Beat*) I'm sorry, Richard.

Richard Why on earth didn't you tell us?

Jan How could I? You had become their father; I couldn't hurt you. And what would have been the point of telling the kids? He'd gone and he wasn't coming back. Why mess up what we had?

Ben Did you reply to any of these letters?

Jan No — never.

Ben How do we know that's true?

Brice It is. She never replied.

Beat

Ben Is there any more?

Jan Yes, there is more.

Brice Come on, Ben.

Jan Like you, Brice, I want it over with once and for all.

Brice It isn't necessary.

Jan Well, I think it is. (*Beat*) Brice's disappearance; it didn't happen in quite the way I've always led you to believe. Or for the same reasons. I asked him to leave. In fact, I threw him out. And there was no other woman.

Brice You didn't tell them that!

Jan I had to tell them something. Anyway, they were far too young; they didn't understand. The truth is — he couldn't settle; he had absolutely no sense of responsibility. He was full of silly pie-in-the-sky ideals; a dreamer with ambitions to become an artist although he couldn't paint; a singer but he couldn't sing for toffee; a musician because, like most people at the time, he had a guitar but he couldn't play it.

Brice Here — hang on ...

Jan You were tone deaf, Brice — come on admit it. Worst of all, he imagined we could all just throw in the towel, ignore all the money we owed, and back-pack round the world and the Lord would provide.

Brice Oddly enough, He usually has. I'm still alive.

Jan The last straw was when he tried to convert me and the kids to Zen Buddhism! It was then I realized I'd married a complete stranger who was going to let us all down. He had to go.

Beat. Silence. No-one knows what to say

I saw him off at Victoria Station one wet and windy Monday morning. He was heading for France then on to God knows where. I asked him not to write or get in touch in any way. When I did receive his letters, I read them then burned them. (*Beat*) And yes, I still loved him. For a while. But then, in time, that died too. And until today I'd even forgotten what he looked like. (*Beat*) There — now you have it.

Silence. Slowly, Ben begins to laugh

Richard Ben ... please ...

The laughter grows louder

Sam This is hysteria setting in. It isn't funny, Ben.

Ben Isn't it? What a bloody mess it all is. (*He stops laughing, and looks at everyone*) So what happens now?

Jan I want you to go, Brice. Thank you for coming: I'm sure you were full of good intentions, but as you can see, we're all perfectly happy.

Brice Happy? After what I've witnessed here today?
Jan Mere trifles, domestic problems, Richard?
Richard Ah, yes; our children have always presented us with our fair share of those, old boy.

Eunice appears on the terrace

Eunice I'm sorry, Jan but I can't keep this coffee warm for ever.
Jan I don't think we shall be needing it, Eunice — our guests are about to depart.

A doorbell rings in the house

Eunice Shall I go ... ?
Jan Would you ...

Eunice exits

Charlie stirs and wakes up during the following

Richard Who on earth's that at this time of night?
Charlie (*sitting up*) Where the hell am I ....?
Jan It's all right, dear — we're here.
Charlie Sorry about that. Was I drunk?
Sam You *are* drunk — and you've missed the big picture, honey. It was a belter.
Charlie What's happened now?
Sam Forget it. Come on, I'll get Miles. We don't want to miss the last ferry. (*She moves towards the house and stops by Brice*) Am I supposed to say I'm sorry?
Brice No. I think that ought to be me, Sam. Anyway, your father's right: none of it matters now.

Sam hesitates for a moment then goes off into the house

Charlie What's she on about? What's been going on?

Eunice appears

Eunice There's a gentleman asking for you, Ben. Says he has something for you.
Ben (*rising*) Ah, yes; I know what that'll be. Give us a hand, Dad.

Richard makes to rise

Not you, Dad — the other one.

Ben and Brice exit with Eunice

Charlie (*getting his shoes*) Right, that's it — we're off then. (*He puts on his shoes*)

Jan Charlie, please think about things — don't do anything rash. Consider carefully, eh?

Charlie Don't nag, Mother; it's my life and I have to do something about it.

Jan I'm sure Ben will sort out your finances if you let him.

Charlie If I do as I'm told, you mean.

Jan It isn't easy, breaking up a family.

Richard Leave the boy alone. Let him decide for himself. (*To Charlie*) Are you keeping those shorts? I'm rather fond of them.

Charlie I'll get Kay to wash them and send them back. (*About Brice*) Is he clearing off or what?

Jan Brice will do as he wishes. He always did. Don't worry, you needn't ever see him again.

Charlie Good! We can forget him then — ponce!

Eunice enters from the house with a tray of coffee and mugs

Eunice Coffee for anyone who needs it. (*She pours a cup*)

Charlie helps himself to coffee

Jan I suppose you heard all that, Eunice.

Eunice No, dear. But I'm afraid Hettie did. She just had to tell me. (*She takes the coffee over to Jan*)

Sam enters from the house with Miles

Sam Go on, then, give Nan and Grandpa a kiss and say thank you.

Miles Must I ... ?

Richard Leave the lad alone, Sam — he doesn't want to kiss his wrinkly old grandad, do you?

Jan (*to Eunice*) Who was at the door?

Eunice A man with dozens of cardboard boxes. A Mr Quincey — I don't know him.

Jan Mr Quincey! Oh, no ...

Ben and Brice enter from the house, each carrying a large box tied with string

Richard What in the world ... ?

Brice (*heading back to the house*) I'll get the rest and see him off.

Brice exits

Richard What are they?
Ben (*kissing the top of Richard's head*) Happy birthday, Pa.
Sam What did I say? The most lavish and the most expensive present is from Ben.

Richard pulls the string off one of the boxes, opens it, and takes out some framed photos of old film stars

Richard (*obviously very moved*) Good Lord! My collection!
Ben We've put your scripts and your books in the den.
Jan How did you manage that?
Ben How many Mr Quinceys are there in Ventnor? I gave him a call and that was that.
Jan But he paid a fortune for it all.
Ben I offered him twice as much — he jumped at it.
Jan Ben ... all that money!
Ben It's only money, Mother. When will you learn?
Richard (*overwhelmed*) I don't know what to say. First the shock of losing them — now the shock of having them returned.
Charlie Don't worry, Dad, he'll look on it as a bloody investment; they'll be his when you've popped your clogs. Nothing for you and me, Sam.
Sam I'm just glad to see them back.
Richard (*excited*) Can I put them up now? And my books back on the shelves. I shall need a hammer and some nails.
Eunice I'll get them — leave it to Eunice.

Eunice and Ben exit into the house

Richard I must be the luckiest man in the world. (*He sits, holding some of the pictures close to his chest*)
Charlie (*kissing Jan*) Right, Mum — we'll leave you to it. See you ... when?
Sam Next year, knowing us. Another party?
Jan No way. No more parties. They wear me out.
Charlie (*to Sam*) Car keys ... ?
Sam I've got them; we don't want you arrested before we reach the ferry.
Charlie Come on, Miles, home time.
Sam (*kissing Richard*) Bye, Dad. I'm very happy for you.
Jan Don't you want to say goodbye to Brice? You may never see him again.
Charlie Yes, and that'll be too soon. (*He kisses Richard*) Bye, Dad. We'll be in touch.

Charlie exits by the back gate with Miles

Sam (*hugging Jan*) Have we all been a pain as usual?
Jan Oh, don't be silly. I just hope the day wasn't ruined for you.
Sam Why did you never tell us all that before?
Jan You know now, so what does it matter? It's over; forget it.
Sam He doesn't seem too bad, I suppose.
Jan Well — at a distance.
Sam Tell him we said goodbye and wish him well.
Jan Really ...?
Sam Well — that we said goodbye at least.

Sam exits by the gate

Jan stands and waves Charlie, Sam and Miles off

Jan (*calling*) And do ring ... write ... come and see us. Please.

We hear a car starting and driving off

Richard (*calling but not moving at all*) Bye, now. Take care.

Silence. Jan closes the gate and comes and puts her arms around Richard's neck

Jan It wasn't too bad I suppose ...
Richard He's such an extravagant boy. (*There are tears in his eyes*) They're all my life amounts to, Jan.
Jan Oh, now ...

Brice comes out of the house

Brice I think they need your expert advice on where to hang the pictures.
Richard (*excitedly*) Ah, yes — now I want them back in exactly the same places ...

Richard picks up the box and heads into the house

(*As he goes*) I want the Clark Gable there — the Spencer Tracy beside it ... and the James Dean ...

Richard exits

Jan and Brice look across at each other. She sits on the lounger

Brice The others gone, have they?
Jan Yes. Peace and quiet at last. What about you?
Brice Ben's just coming. In time for the last ferry, are we?

Jan (*looking at her watch*) Just. (*Beat*) It's been a long day.
Brice Do you think I'm forgiven?
Jan By the kids? Who can say? Only time will tell.
Brice And we haven't much of that left.
Jan Speak for yourself.
Brice (*taking a last look at the "view"*) At least you haven't wasted your life. I can see that now.
Jan And you have — is that it?
Brice I don't know. I shall be leaving next week. Back to the life I'm used to. But at least I'll be able to picture you here, doing the garden perhaps, chatting to Eunice, sitting out here in the sunshine. Or in the winter maybe, in front of a roaring fire in the den, Richard's collection back in place.
Jan It was your decision, Brice.
Brice You still see it that way, do you?
Jan Yes. Blame me if it suits you. I don't mind.
Brice (*moving up to her*) You asked why I came back. It was watching Barnaby, lying there, helpless, talking about old times, wondering if each day might be his last, Rose nursing him knowing it was useless — it made me suddenly aware of my own mortality.

Beat

Ben comes out of the house, his jacket over his shoulder

Ben Fit?
Brice Whenever you are.
Ben He's dead chuffed in there. Eunice is helping him unpack the boxes. No bed for him tonight. (*He kisses Jan on the cheek*) You OK ... ?
Jan I'm fine. But no more shocks, Ben. Drive safely.
Ben (*heading for the gate*) I'll start the car, Dad.
Jan Ben. (*He stops and turns to her*) Your friend. Why not bring him down. We'd love to meet him.
Ben (*after a moment*) We'll see, shall we ... ? Bye for now.

Ben exits

Brice It doesn't bother you?
Jan Ben? Why should it? I wish he'd felt able to tell us himself — but one can't have everything. I just want he and Charlie to be friends again.
Brice Do you mind if I keep in touch? Only now and then — a postcard, nothing more. Just in case.

Jan remains silent

You never know. You may need a friend one day. (*He extends his hand*) Bye.

Jan (*not moving at all*) We said goodbye a long time ago, Brice. Victoria
Station — remember?
Brice (*quietly*) *Au revoir*, Princess.

Brice turns and leaves through the gate

Ben (*off, calling*) Dad ... Dad ... ?

We hear another car starting up and leaving

Jan is left alone

We hear the sound of nails being hammered into a wall in the den

Eunice enters from the house

Eunice He's getting bossy in there, Jan. (*She sits and pours herself some
coffee*)
Jan Best leave him — he's happy.

*Hettie comes out of the house wearing her dressing-gown, and with a hot
drink in her hand*

Hettie I suppose we're going to have this wretched knocking all night. (*She
sits*) All gone, have they?

No-one answers

Anything I can do ... ?

Jan rises, goes to the terrace, picks up the watering can and waters the plants

The music we heard at the beginning of the scene starts to creep in

The Lights slowly fade

The music grows louder. Black-out

FURNITURE AND PROPERTY LIST

ACT I

On stage: Shrubs
Plants, including agapanthus
Hanging baskets
Long wooden table
Smaller table
Benches
Chairs
Lounger
Watering can
Local newspaper
Ashtray
"The Times" crossword for **Richard**
Book for **Hettie**

Off stage: Tablecloth and jug of flowers (**Jan**)
Box containing cake (**Eunice**)
Tray with jug, Pimms, lemonade, ice, fruit, glasses (**Eunice**)
Football (**Stage Management**)
Bag. *In it*: can of soft drink, packet of cigarettes, lighter, pack of cards
    (**Sam**)
Lettuce (**Jan**)
Can of beer (**Charlie**)
Fruit flan, can of hair spray, dress (**Eunice**)
Two large bowls of salad (**Eunice**)
Plates and other crockery (**Jan**)
Bottles of red wine (2) and white wine (2) (**Eunice**)
Wine glasses (**Jan**)
Glasses, napkins, cutlery (**Jan** and **Eunice**)
Several birthday presents (**Charlie**)
Bread and knife (**Eunice**)
Mobile house phone (**Richard**)
Another can of beer (**Charlie**)
Bowl of fruit (**Eunice**)
Bottle of mineral water (**Hettie**)
Wrapped presents (**Sam**)
Wrapped copy of "Chronicle of the Cinema" (**Miles**)
Bottle of champagne, bouquet of flowers (**Ben**)
Tray of puddings (**Eunice**)

During lighting change p.18:

Set: Cards for **Hettie** and **Miles**

Personal: **Jan**: watch (worn throughout)
                Charlie: handkerchief

ACT II

Strike: Everything from main table except bowl of fruit

Off stage: Glass of wine (**Ben**)
                Mug of tea (**Eunice**)
                Another can of beer (**Charlie**)
                Glass of wine and can of beer (**Ben**)
                Suitcase, headscarf, pair of gloves (**Hettie**)
                Tray of coffee and mugs (**Eunice**)
                Two large boxes tied with string, one containing framed
                    photos of old film stars (**Ben** and **Brice**)
                Jacket (**Ben**)
                Hot drink (**Hettie**)

Personal: Hand-rolled cigarette, lighter (**Brice**)
                Packet of cigarettes, lighter (**Sam**)

During lighting change p. 57:

Re-set: Empty wine bottles, glasses etc. littering table

LIGHTING PLOT

Practical fittings required: nil
1 exterior. The same throughout

ACT I

To open: Brilliant sunshine

Cue 1   **Hettie**: "Not for me — thank you ... !"   (Page 18)
         Fade to black-out

Cue 2   When ready   (Page 18)
         Bring up lights to opening position

Cue 3   **Eunice**: "Ice-cream, anyone, trifle ...?"   (Page 36)
         Fade quickly to black-out

ACT II

To open: Sunshine, but now from lower in the sky

Cue 4   Music grows louder   (Page 57)
         Fade slowly to black-out

Cue 5   When ready   (Page 57)
         Bring up lights on evening setting

Cue 6   Music creeps in   (Page 72)
         Slowly fade lights

Cue 7   Music grows louder   (Page 72)
         Black-out

EFFECTS PLOT

ACT I

Cue 1   As play begins   (Page 1)
          Distant sound of the sea and seagulls (continuous)

Cue 2   **Charlie**: "Blissfully ignorant."   (Page 13)
          Bring up seagull sound slightly

Cue 3   Lights fade   (Page 18)
          Music

Cue 4   Establish **Miles** and **Hettie** playing cards   (Page 18)
          Fade music

Cue 5   **Sam**: " ... you can't deny that."   (Page 24)
          Telephone rings

Cue 6   **Sam**: "Why are you so jumpy?"   (Page 24)
          Cut phone during following conversation

ACT II

Cue 7   As ACT II begins   (Page 37)
          Distant sound of the sea and seagulls (continuous)

Cue 8   **Jan**: "I need a moment to myself."   (Page 57)
          Popular sixties' tune from house

Cue 9   **Jan**: "— life is different for you ..."   (Page 57)
          Increase volume of music; play from auditorium speakers

Cue 10   Establish cast dancing   (Page 57)
          Switch to Manfred Mann: "Pretty Flamingo"

Cue 11   Cast make sounds for when sex is in the air   (Page 58)
          Cut music

Cue 12   **Jan**: " ... our guests are about to depart."   (Page 67)
          Doorbell

Cue 13   **Jan**: " ... come and see us. Please."   (Page 70)
          Car starting and driving off

Cue 14   **Ben** (*off*): "Dad ... Dad ... ?"   (Page 72)
          *Car starting and leaving. Pause. Sound of nails being
              hammered into a wall*

Cue 15   **Jan** waters the plants   (Page 72)
          Music

Cue 16   Lights fade   (Page 72)
          Increase volume of music